Tangible
press

BLOWN OUT
ON
THE TRAIL

20 YEARS OF UNRELEASED BOB DYLAN RECORDINGS

JOHN HOWELLS

Printed in the United States of America

First Printing, 2019

ISBN-13: 978-1-7323892-9-8

This book is dedicated to the memory of Peter Stone Brown
— 1951-2019

"The only truth is music."
— Jack Kerouac

"Music is a language that doesn't speak in particular words. It speaks in emotions, and if it's in the bones, it's in the bones."
— Keith Richards

"Information is not knowledge. Knowledge is not wisdom. Wisdom is not truth. Truth is not beauty. Beauty is not love. Love is not music. Music is THE BEST."
— Frank Zappa

Table of Contents

Introduction

This is the second volume in the *Skipping Reels of Rhyme* series, the first of which covered the years 1958 through 1975. This volume picks up where that one left off, starting with the second half of the Rolling Thunder Revue in 1976 and continuing through 1996. This two-decade period was an extremely active one for Bob Dylan, with constant touring and numerous recording sessions, as well as appearances at all-star events such as Live Aid and Farm Aid, but all of this activity amounted to very little creatively as compared to his pre-1976 years. I would consider this to be his "lost in the wilderness" years. During this time he experienced the dissolution of his ten-year marriage, followed by his conversion to Christianity, followed by years of confusion over which direction he was taking. Along the way, he found himself taking part in numerous projects where he was a mere participant (although a very celebrated and important one) rather than the lead instigator. Certainly there was some of that in the 1960s, but it seems he did a lot more of that in the time period covered here. He released some great music during this time, but also some of his very worst (according to many fans). All of this will be covered, hopefully, in some detail.

In documenting all of this, it is my aim to tell a story along the way. I will attempt to speculate from time to time about possible motives, although there is a great deal of documentation in the way of interviews and writings from various sources, which I certainly borrow from, but even if the words come out of Dylan's own mouth, we can never really be sure of the truth. My real goal here is to review the various unreleased and rare live and studio material that has been traded by fans for many years and talk very subjectively about the sound quality, as well as musical quality, and give my best recommendations for what to seek out.

13

There are two things that occur in this period of time that separates it from the previous two decades. First of all, live and unreleased recordings from the 1960s and early 1970s were somewhat rare due to the primitive nature of home recording devices and the equally primitive method of sharing what few rare tapes were in circulation among collectors. In addition, in the early years of the young Bob Dylan performing and recording, it was not all that clear to the public at large that he would become the household name he has since become, and so the impetus to go to the trouble of hauling a massive reel-to-reel tape recorder to a show was pretty low. Consequently, the number of rare recordings from the early years is extremely limited. However, starting with the 1974 tour with The Band and the first leg of the Rolling Thunder Revue, portable tape cassette recorders were more common and easier to smuggle into a gig. Therefore, collectors experienced a plethora of great recordings from that time period. Not only live recordings but studio recordings as well were starting to get out into circulation, so thus began the period where virtually everything he recorded in the studio or performed live was somehow captured by someone somewhere. From 1976 to 1996, the period this book is interested in, recording quality improved tremendously, up to the point where digital recordings became the norm. The second thing of importance is the nature of "tape trading", whereby Dylan collectors throughout the world once swapped cassette tapes or bootleg vinyl, the standard in the late '90s was digital trading through FTP servers and other file sharing systems. Now you could instantly find the music you were looking for, if you knew where to look. Pretty much the only people who could do this at the time were computer professionals and college students with access to lab computers. By 1996, we had the World Wide Web, which opened up the Internet to the average consumer, and today we have bit torrent servers allowing a wide circle of Bob Dylan enthusiasts to share the latest shows almost as soon as the band left the stage.

All of this led to an overload of Dylan recordings in the 1980s and beyond. It is not the intention of this book to discuss in detail each and every unreleased recording, live or otherwise, because there is just too much to choose from. Instead, I will talk about the studio outtakes that are in actual circulation, as long as they are significantly different from what is available on the official albums, and live appearances that are of an unexpected or otherwise special nature, but for each year of touring I will suggest several of what I consider to be the best sounding, best performances, or most unusual, and will discuss why I believe them to be worthy of special interest to collectors. For the novice, the big question may be "where can I find these recordings?" The answer will vary. Access to social media allows new collectors to connect with other collectors who may have access to something rare and unusual. The Internet, in general, is a good place to look, but I won't tell you where. The fun is finding out for yourself!

Blown Out on the Trail

Notes

There are various categories of recordings, sometimes in the form of magnetic tape and more often these days in the form of some sort of digital medium, be it CD, CD-R, MP3 or FLAC files, etc. They all have something in common: they come from a particular source that could be one of several things. Here are some things to look for.

PA – Refers to the Public Address system, which is basically the mixed output from a live concert sent to the massive speakers every concert hall or club uses to that you can actually hear what is happening. From the microphone right to your ears with no audience interference in-between. For the purposes of this book a PA recording is defnied as a professional recording made for the purpose of putting together a live album or for publishing demos of certain songs. The best PA recordings will rival any professional live album you could buy in a store, though your mileage may vary.

Soundboard – Often used interchangeably with PA, but more often the case it is not always properly mixed, but it is a direct line from the mixing board to the PA system. A recording said to be from the soundboard is usually made by someone in the road crew, often for the purpose of having a personal copy to save or for the purpose of the artist to listen to as a reference. It could also refer to a tap off of one or more monitor mixes. These are sources that are useful for the musicians during their performance in order to allow them to more closely hear what they are doing or what other specific instruments are doing. Monitor mixes can sometimes sound jarringly off if the monitor being sampled only contains vocals or only contains certain instruments. As is often the case, the origin of the various soundboards is unknown and the quality will vary.

Audience – As you might expect, the source is from a portable recording device used by someone in the audience. Audience recordings, are of course, surreptitious and could easily be confiscated by the staff at a venue, so they are stealthy and not intended to be used for any sort of professional use. The best audience recordings are made using the highest quality DAT or cassette recorders and placed in a location where there is not a whole lot of crowd chatter. The worst audience recordings will have some loudmouth lout standing right next to the recorder yelling out requests or any number of chattering morons who didn't come to hear the music but instead came to hear themselves talk. The quality of the sound itself could be great, but an unruly audience can ruin an otherwise great recording. In other cases, the crowd noise could be minimal, but the placement of the device is just too far away from the speakers to be of any use. What can really make a great audience tape worthwhile, however, is the balance of instruments with voices and a nice stereo separation with a nice tone: not too much bass and not too much treble.

Pre-board – A fairly useless term that does come up from time to time. It almost always refers to monitor mixes taken by someone with access to the sound system, i.e. someone tapping into the source between the mixing board and the stage monitors. There are a large number of these from the 1993 leg of the Never Ending Tour, and the consensus is that they were made by a member of the road crew and only came into circulation once that person had passed away. Pre-boards are rare and not always that desirable, although you do have the advantage of hearing the music without any discernable audience noise present.

And now a word about sound quality:

I prefer a five-step rating system, typically used by book and record collectors to grade physical condition rather than aesthetic concerns. Not a number system, the ratings are: "poor", "fair", "good", "very good", and "excellent". When grading physical condition, excellent is usually replaced with "mint" or "near mint", but this obviously doesn't apply to rating sound quality, so "excellent" it is. I'll try to give some criteria for my ratings.

Note: studio tapes include soundboard (or PA), album sessions and studio outtakes, radio & TV broadcasts, home/apartment/party tapes, etc. Audience tapes include amateur concert recordings, open-mike recordings from a TV speaker or studio playback speakers (yes, there are such things!), rehearsal and soundcheck tapes from a distance, etc.

The ratings can mean different things depending on the source of the recording. For instance, a poor studio tape is very different from a poor audience recording. By its very nature, a studio tape is expected to sound much better than something recorded from a noisy audience on sometimes inferior audio equipment. The studio tape has the advantage of being recorded with (presumably) state of the art gear, and so if the resulting tape is poor sounding it must *really* be bad, i.e. somehow damaged or copied too many times or distorted or whatever. The audience tape, on the other hand, never really had a chance to begin with, and a decent sounding tape made under these circumstances will no doubt be judged less harshly. An excellent audience tape can still have a few flaws which would not be tolerated with a studio recording, but given the circumstances those flaws are excused if the sound is overwhelmingly good and nothing really distracts from the enjoyment of the music. There are really very few truly "excellent" audio tapes around, but there are many that come close enough to be given that rating anyway. Most studio tapes in circulation are what would be rated as excellent, and a rating of "good" for a studio tape is actually a backhanded compliment. If it's only "good" and not "excellent", then there must be something wrong with it.

My ratings and qualifications:

Poor: For an audience recording, a rating of *poor* means that the tape or CD is virtually unlistenable. This could be because the audience is much too loud, the music is too far away from the recording device, there is too much distortion, or any number of other problems. In any case, it's painful to try to listen to and ultimately turns out to be an exercise in futility. Only the most historically significant recordings with this rating are worthwhile. For a studio recording, *poor* means that it actually sounds worse than the worst audience tape. With a poor audience tape you might at least be able to get some of the ambience of the concert, but with a poor studio tape you just have garbage. The "party tapes" deserve more leeway because it's presumed that the equipment used isn't really studio quality. Since I don't have any CDs that would rate as *poor*, I can't give any examples, but there are many vinyl boots from the early days that would rate *poor*, including much of the classic *Great White Wonder*.

Fair: Means that there is a lot of audience noise and chatter but at least the music can be heard fairly well. Generally a solid enough recording, but only good enough to fill the gap until a better one comes along. The recording level is probably a little low, resulting in a fair amount of hiss, or the level could be too high, resulting in some distortion. Audience noise is a big factor in my ratings. If the sound of the music is loud and clear with a nice balance between bass and treble, and yet there is some asshole yelling his ass off for "Desolation Rowwwwwww!!!" throughout the performance very near the mike, it *won't* rank very highly with me. Another qualification for anything above *fair* would be the tone and balance of the music itself. If a full band, the bass should be loud and clear - but not enough to drown out other instruments - and there should be a good balance between the high and low end. If this isn't satisfactory, it would rate *fair* at a minumum. In fact, most *fair* audience recordings have a dull sound to them and seem to be lacking in bass or treble. I don't think studio recordings (other than party tapes) would rate *fair*. If they're not *good* then they're *poor*. Most concert bootleg lps from the '70s would would receive a *fair* rating.

Good: Most present day audience recordings would fall into this category. This means that the audience is noisy and intrusive at times, but the music is clearly heard and bass, guitars, drums, keyboards, and voice(s) are all well blended and sound reasonably crisp. There will be some flaws here and there, such as an occasional dropout of one channel, or maybe a poor edit or incomplete song or two, but the flaws don't detract from the generally good sound quality. Recording level is loud but not distorted. Overall, a very decent addition to anyone's collection. A studio recording with a *good* rating would probably mean lots of hiss and some occasional wobbles, and maybe a bit of distortion here and there, but all in all a good sounding tape or CD. Example: *All the Way Down To Italy* (CD).

Very good: An otherwise excellent audience tape or CD only slightly spoiled by some audience noise during the quieter moments, or static or tape transport problems resulting in brief moments of inferior sound. Generally, *very good* is what an *excellent* tape or CD would sound like if only that guy three rows back would stop whistling every time Dylan ends a chorus of "It Ain't Me Babe", as if it were some sort of massive achievement. All instruments are clear and well balanced. The voice is right upfront and there is absolutely no distortion and very little (if any) hiss. *Very good* studio tapes are just one official release shy of perfection. Some hiss, but not so much that you'd really notice unless you deliberately went out of your way to listen for it. Examples: most of the '92 and '93 audience recordings found on CD would rank *very good*. These are otherwise excellent DAT sources that have a little too much audience presence for my liking. Also, *Before the Crash I & II* would probably rank *very good* because of the vinyl crackling heard throughout – unavoidable because of the original acetates used as a source.

Excellent: The Holy Grail of audience recordings. I have quite a few audience recordings that I rank *excellent*, but truthfully only a very few actually deserve it. An excellent audience recording has

21

absolutely no audience presence at all, or at least very little – so little that you really have a hard time telling the difference between audience and soundboard. Occasionally an excellent audience tape will sound *better* than an equivalent soundboard. No one can be heard yelling out requests; applause sounds as if it's coming from someplace other than next to the tape recorder; no coughing; no comments on the songs or performance from instant rock critics; and the tone of the instruments is nothing short of glorious. Studio/soundboard tapes/CDs are ready for release, with no flaws whatsoever. In fact, some labels like KTS and Swinging Pig have actually gone out of their way to try to correct perceived flaws to create a release-ready product that rivals in every way anything that CBS-SONY could ever hope to do. Some examples would include: *Stuck Inside of New York, Wanted Man, Now Ain't the Time For Your Tears, Manchester Prayer*, etc.

A Bob Dylan Timeline 1976-1996

January 5, 1976 – *Desire* released. Critical reaction was extremely positive. Reached #1 in the US.

January 27, 1976 – Appearance at Joni Mitchell concert in Austin, Texas. Performs "Girl from the North Country" with Joni. No known tape exists.

April 18, 1976 – Second half of the Rolling Thunder tour begins in Lakeland, Florida.

April 22, 1976 – Taping for a proposed TV special in Clearwater, Florida. It was scrapped in favor of later performances from Fort Worth, Texas and Fort Collins, Colorado.

March 30, 1976 – First recording session with Eric Clapton for the *No Reason To Cry* album, performing the new Dylan song "Sign Language".

September 14, 1976 – NBC-TV broadcasts the special *Hard Rain*. Features performances from Fort Worth and Fort Collins.

November 25, 1976 – Appears as a guest at The Band's farewell concert at Winterland in San Francisco. Performs several songs with The Band, only a few of which made it to the final film.

March 1977 – Recording session for Leonard Cohen's album *Death of a Ladies Man*.

January 25, 1978 – The movie *Renaldo and Clara* was released to almost universal negative reviews. Sometime later, the four-hour version of the film was edited down to a two-hour version. The film remains unreleased on home video.

February 20, 1978 – World tour begins in Tokyo.

April 1978 – Release of the film *The Last Waltz*. Directed by Martin Scorsese.

April 25, 1978 – *Street Legal* sessions begin.

June 15, 1978 – *Street Legal* released. Reached #11 in the US and #2 in the UK.

August 21, 1978 – *Live at Budokan* released, initially only in Japan on the Sony label. Critical reaction was poor. It would later see a US release on Columbia Records.

April 30, 1979 – *Slow Train Coming* sessions begin.

August 28, 1979 – *Slow Train Coming* released. Critical reaction was mostly positive and it was his best selling album since *Desire*. Reached #3 in the US and #2 in the UK.

October 20, 1979 – Appears on *Saturday Night Live* performing "Gotta Serve Somebody", "I Believe in You", and "When You Gonna Wake Up".

November 1, 1979 – First gospel tour begins.

January 11, 1980 – Second gospel tour begins.

February 11, 1980 – *Saved* sessions begin.

February 27, 1980 – Appearance on the Grammy Awards ceremony. Bob performs and wins for Best Male Rock Vocal performance for "Gotta Serve Somebody".

April 17, 1980 – Third gospel tour begins.

June 23, 1980 – *Saved* released. Critical reception was mixed. Album reached #24 in the US and #3 in the UK.

November 9, 1980 – Musical Retrospective tour begins. Bob begins to add older songs back into the mix.

March 3, 1981 – *Shot of Love* sessions begin.

June 10, 1981 – The last gospel tour begins.

August 10, 1981 – *Shot of Love* released. Critical reaction was poor. It reached #33 in the US and #6 in the UK. It was his poorest showing in the charts since his debut album.

February 23, 1982 – Session for Allen Ginsburg's album *Holy Soul Jelly Roll — Poems and Songs.*

June 1, 1982 – Clydie King session. Bob plays instruments (guitar, organ, bass) but does not sing, apparently. There is no tape circulating, so no one can know for sure.

June 2, 1982 – Peace Sunday Rally. Sings a few songs with Joan Baez.

February 16, 1983 – Guest appearance at Rick Danko/Levon Helm show at the Lone Star Café in New York City.

April 11, 1983 – *Infidels* sessions begin.

November 1, 1983 – *Infidels* released. Reached #20 in the US and #9 in the UK. Critical reception was mostly positive and helped to rehabilitate his reputation somewhat.

March 22, 1984 – Appears on *Late Nite with David Letterman* with the Plugz. Plays songs from *Infidels.*

May 28, 1984 – European tour begins in Verona, Italy.

July 24, 1984 – Al Green session. Sings backup on a few songs.

July 26, 1984 – *Empire Burlesque* sessions begin.

September 1984 – Lone Justice session for *The World Is Not My Home* album.

December 3, 1984 – Live album *Real Live* released. It was his lowest selling album to date, reaching #115 in the US and #54 in the UK.

April 1985 – Sly Dunbar & Robbie Shakespeare recording session. Plays harmonica on "No Name on the Bullet".

June 8, 1985 – *Empire Burlesque* released. Critical reception was generally positive and sales were much better than the previous album with #33 in the US and #11 in the UK. Most fans, though, despised the post-production which included many overdubs and synthesizers that were considered too commercial.

July 13, 1985 – Live Aid concert. Performs acoustically with Keith Richards and Ron Wood.

September 22, 1985 – Farm Aid concert. Plays live with Tom Petty and the Heartbreakers for the first time.

November 7, 1985 – *Biograph* released. The 5-LP set contained many rarities and previously unreleased songs.

January 26, 1986 – All-star celebration for Martin Luther King, Jr. Performs "I Shall Be Released" and "Blowin' in the Wind".

February 5, 1986 – *True Confessions* tour with Tom Petty and the Heartbreakers begins.

February 9, 1986 – Sessions for *Band of the Hand* single.

February 19, 1986 – Appears at a Dire Straits concert and performs four songs with the band.

April 18, 1986 – *Knocked out Loaded* sessions begin.

June 6, 1986 – Plays with Tom Petty and the Heartbreakers at the Amnesty International concert.

June 1986 – HBO special *Hard to Handle* airs.

July 14, 1986 – *Knocked out Loaded* released to extremely poor critical reception. Reached #53 in the US and #35 in the UK. It is widely regarded as one of his very worst albums.

August 27, 1986 – *Hearts of Fire* sessions begin.

November 10, 1986 – Bob presents the Canadian Music Hall of Fame Juno award for Gordon Lightfoot in Toronto.

February 19, 1987 – Guest appearance at a Taj Mahal concert, along with George Harrison and John Fogerty.

February 1987 – Warren Zevon recording session for the *Sentimental Hygiene* album. Plays harmonica on "The Factory".

March 5, 1987 – *Down in the Groove* sessions begin.

March 11, 1987 – George Gershwin Celebration Concert. Performs an acoustic version of the Gershwin tune "Soon".

April 14, 1987 – Ringo Starr recording session. Plays harmonica on "Wish I Know Now What I Knew Then".

April 20, 1987 – Appearance at U2 concert in Los Angeles. Performs "I Shall Be Released" and "Knockin' on Heaven's Door".

June 1987 – U2 recording session for *Rattle and Hum* album. Sings with Bono on "Love Rescue Me".

July 4, 1987 – First concert with the Grateful Dead in Foxboro, Massachusetts.

September 5, 1987 – *Temples in Flames* tour with Tom Petty and the Heartbreakers begins.

October 9, 1987 – *Hearts of Fire* film and soundtrack released. Dylan has since disowned the film.

January 20, 1988 – Rock & Roll Hall of Fame induction and concert.

May 7, 1988 – First Traveling Wilburys session.

May 29, 1988 – Appearance at Levon Helm concert at the Lone Star Café in New York City.

May 30, 1988 – *Down in the Groove* released, again to poor critical reception. It reached #61 in the US and #32 in the UK. Most fans consider it one of his worst.

June 7, 1988 – *Never Ending Tour* begins in Concord, California.

October 18, 1988 – *Traveling Wilburys Volume One* released. With the presence of superstars like George Harrison, Roy Orbison, and

Tom Petty, the reception was enthusiastic and reached #3 in the US and #16 in the UK.

December 4, 1988 – Bridge School Concert in Oakland, California. An acoustic performance with G. E. Smith.

February 6, 1989 – *Dylan and the Dead* live album released. It was generally poorly received and only reached #37 in the US and #38 in the UK.

February 12, 1989 – Guest appearance with the Grateful Dead in Los Angeles. Bob mostly just plays guitar and sings one song.

February 28, 1989 – *Oh Mercy* sessions begin.

June 27, 1989 – Filming for the Van Morrison TV special *One Irish Rover*.

September 19, 1989 – *Oh Mercy* released. It was hailed by critics and fans alike and led to a brief resurgence in popularity. It reached #30 in the US and #6 in the UK.

September 24, 1989 – Chabad Telethon appearance. Performs with Peter Himmelman and Harry Dean Stanton.

November 20, 1989 – Recording for the *Flashback* soundtrack. Records "People Get Ready".

January 1990 – Brian Wilson recording session for aborted album *Sweet Insanity*. The song was "The Spirit of Rock and Roll".

January 6, 1990 – *Under the Red Sky* sessions begin.

January 12, 1990 – Appearance at Toad's Place in New Haven. Longest concert of the Never Ending Tour.

January 30, 1990 – Dylan accepts *Le France Commandeur Ordre Des Arts Et Des Lettres* in Paris, France.

February 24, 1990 – Roy Orbison tribute in Los Angeles.

April 1990 – Traveling Wilburys sessions for the second album.

September 11, 1990 – *Under the Red Sky* released. It was not well received, unfairly I believe. It reached #38 in the US and #13 in the UK.

January 1991 – Records "This Old Man" for the *For Our Children* album.

March 26, 1991 – *The Bootleg Series Volumes 1-3* was released. This was the first in a series of releases focused on rare and previously unreleased recordings.

September 15, 1991 – Appears with Kinky Friedman at the Chabad Telethon. Plays electric guitar on "Sold American".

October 17, 1991 – Appearance at the Guitar Greats Festival in Seville, Spain.

January 18, 1992 – Appears on David Letterman's 10th Anniversary show performing "Like a Rolling Stone" with an all-star band.

June 3, 1992 – Recording sessions for an album produced by David Bromberg begin. The album was never released.

July 1992 – Recording sessions for *Good As I Been to You* in Dylan's garage begin.

October 16, 1992 – "Bobfest", all-star 30th anniversary celebration takes place in New York City.

October 19, 1992 – Recording session with Willie Nelson for the album *Across the Borderline*. Bob duets on "Heartland", which was co-written with Willie Nelson.

October 30, 1992 – *Good As I Been to You* released. It was the first all-acoustic solo album since *Another Side of Bob Dylan* in 1964 and was well received by fans and critics, but only reached #51 in the US and #18 in the UK.

January 13, 1993 – Appearance on the TV broadcast *A Country Music Celebration* with Willie Nelson. Sings "Heartland" with Willie Nelson.

January 17, 1993 – Appearance at Bill Clinton's Presidential inauguration celebration. Later participated in *The Absolutely Unofficial Blue Jeans Bash* the same evening.

January 1993 – Session with Carlene Carter for the *Sweet Meant to Be* album. Sings backup on "Trust Yourself".

February 6, 1993 – Appearance at Van Morrison concert in Dublin. Plays harmonica on "It's All Over Now, Baby Blue".

April 27, 1993 – Filming begins for the Willie Nelson 60th birthday celebration to be broadcast in May. Performs "Hard Times" with his touring band and duets with Willie Nelson on "Pancho and Lefty".

May 19, 1993 – Recording session with Mike Seeger for the album *Third Annual Farewell Reunion*.

May 1993 – Sessions for *World Gone Wrong* begin in Dylan's garage.

August 1993 – *The 30th Anniversary Concert Celebration* is released.

October 24, 1993 – *World Gone Wrong* released. It was his second solo acoustic album in a row. Well received by critics but not a big seller. Reached #70 in the US and #35 in the UK.

November 16-17, 1993 – Supper Club shows in New York City. These shows were supposedly originally intended for *MTV Unplugged*.

November 18, 1993 – Appearance on the David Letterman show. Performs "Forever Young" acoustically with his touring band.

December 1993 – Recording session with Stevie Nicks for the *Street Angel* album. Plays guitar and harmonica on "Just Like a Woman".

March 23, 1994 – Appearance at *The Rhythm, Country & Blues Concert* broadcast March 30.

May 9, 1994 – Recording sessions begin for the album *Till the Night Is Gone: A Tribute to Doc Pomus.*

May 20-22, 1994 – Appearance at *The Great Music Experience* in Nara, Japan. Sings four songs with an orchestra.

August 14, 1994 – Appears with his touring band at the 25th anniversary Woodstock concert.

September 30, 1994 – Recording session in New York City. Sings three rock and roll covers for what purpose, I don't know. Not in general circulation.

October 17, 1994 – Guest appearance at a Grateful Dead concert in New York City singing "Rainy Day Women #12 & 35".

November 15, 1994 – Sessions for *MTV Unplugged* begin.

April 11, 1995 – *MTV Unplugged* European version is released. This version contains bonus tracks not available in the US.

May 5, 1995 – US version of *MTV Unplugged* is released. There was mixed reaction with some fans thinking it was a sell-out. It was his best selling album in a long time, reaching #23 in the US and #10 in the UK.

September 2, 1995 – Appears with his touring band at the Opening of the Rock and Roll Hall of Fame Museum in Cleveland, Ohio.

November 19, 1995 – Appearance at the Frank Sinatra 80th birthday celebration performing "Restless Farewell" with his touring band.

December 1995 – Recording session with Gerry Goffin for the *Back Room Blood* album.

January 1996 – Records "Ring of Fire" for the soundtrack to the film *Feeling Minnesota*.

February 2, 1996 – Performs with his touring band at a private corporate event in Phoenix, Arizona. No recording circulates.

February 1996 – Recording session with Ron Wood. Plays guitar on "Interfere".

"Some of these bootleggers, they make pretty good stuff."

-- Bob Dylan ("Sugar Baby")

Blown Out on the Trail

Rolling Thunder Revue 1976

The second half of the Rolling Thunder Revue in 1976 took a slightly different approach than the first half in 1975, which concentrated mostly on New England and Canada. Where the first leg of the tour had a more intimate and relaxed feel, with the shows mostly confined to medium-sized halls and the shows sometimes being given short notice, the 1976 portion moved to the South and Midwest in larger venues, such as large halls or stadiums.

The second half started in Lakeland, Florida on April 18, after the rehearsals in Clearwater. The tour continued throughout the South and moved West until ending in Salt Lake City, Utah, on May 25. The tour was cut short at that time, most likely due to dwindling ticket sales. Supposedly, the Salt Lake show was only half full and there is no circulating recording. But another reason for the end of the tour could have been that the vibe was just not the same as for the first half. It seems that in 1975 Dylan may have been attempting to recreate the look and feel of the New York City coffee house years by recruiting his fellow folkies for a ragtag band of Gypsies quite unlike the thundering tour he just got through doing with The Band. Having the tour play large venues similar to what he played in 1974 may have been too stressful. I think the whole point of the tour in the first place was to go in the opposite direction of the 1974 tour. Instead of a tightly controlled set of shows that emphasized stellar musicianship and collaboration, the idea may have been to keep it loose and somewhat improvisational. Once a tour becomes too unwieldy, it can lead to stagnation. That may have been what Dylan and company were experiencing toward the end of the road.

The format of the 1976 revue was pretty much as follows: a set of songs performed by various members of the Revue, known informally as Guam, usually in this order: Bob Neuwirth, Steven Soles, T-Bone Burnett, Rob Stoner, Mick Ronson, Donna Weiss, Kinky Friedman. Then Bob took the stage and performed a few solo acoustic songs. Then Bob and the entire band took the stage and performed three or four fully electric songs. After a break, other members of the Revue performed songs without Bob, including Joni Mitchell, Roger McGuinn, and Joan Baez. Bob returned to the stage to perform a short duet set with Joan Baez, and finally a much longer set with Bob and the band, usually ending with "Gotta Travel On".

There are several rehearsal tapes circulating which are of great interest to fans of this tour, and even to non-fans such as myself. Before I go into more detail about the actual concerts themselves, I would like to start by talking about the known rehearsal tapes.

Rehearsals for the second Hurricane Carter Benefit concert
Instrumental Rentals Studio Rehearsals
Los Angeles, California – January 22-23, 1976

Personnel:

Bob Dylan - guitar, harmonica & vocal
Scarlet Rivera - violin
T-bone Burnett - guitar & piano
Steven Soles - guitar
Mick Ronson - guitar
Bobby Neuwirth - guitar & vocal
Roger McGuinn - guitar & vocal
David Mansfield - steel guitar, mandolin, violin & dobro
Rob Stoner - bass
Howie Wyeth - drums
Gary Burke - percussion
Joan Baez - vocal
Rick Danko (special guest) - vocal

The tape contains some songs that Dylan doesn't seem to appear on. The songs that Dylan does appear to be on are:

You Ain't Goin' Nowhere
One More Cup of Coffee
Oh, Sister
Sara
Mozambique
Just Like a Woman
When I Paint My Masterpiece
Maggie's Farm
One Too Many Mornings
Romance in Durango
Isis
Positively 4th Street
Oh, Sister
Sara
Hurricane
Lay Lady Lay

In preparation for the second "Night of the Hurricane" benefit concert, a couple of rehearsals took place. In the first rehearsal on January 22, Dylan's vocals can barely be heard. The second, and much longer rehearsal tape allows us to hear him and we can hear the musicians working out new arrangements to songs previously performed in 1975 as well as new songs that were not attempted during the first part of the tour. These new songs include "Maggie's Farm", "I Threw It All Away", and "Positively 4th Street", the latter of which was performed only at the Hurricane Carter benefit in Houston. "Maggie's Farm" has an arrangement that is close to the *Hard Rain* live version, but with some subtle differences. "One More Cup of Coffee" is particularly effective here, but unfortunately most of the Dylan songs on the Rolling Thunder tour tended to sound the same. At times there is very little variation in the players' techniques, which gives the entire tour a sort of plodding sameness that gets tiresome at times. The band is actually

39

very good, though, and you can really hear that in the Roger McGuinn and Joan Baez sets. I think the problem was that the band really didn't know how to handle Bob's music as well as their own or others. If anyone is at fault here, it's Bob himself. That said, however, there are some high spots that I will get to later when discussing the recommended shows.

Songs on the tape that don't appear to involve Dylan are:

Loving You is Sweeter than Ever
Mad Man
It Makes No Difference
Instrumental
Ride 'Em Jewboy
Eating Ice-chrome at a Spaceball Game
Silver Mantis

Songs 1 and 3 are sung by Rick Danko. I am not aware if he appeared at the concert on January 25.

CDs:
- **Days before the Hurricane (Come One! Come All!)**
- **Going Going Guam**

Clearwater Rehearsals
Belleview Biltmore Hotel
Clearwater, Florida – April 12-17, 1976

Personnel:

Bob Dylan - guitar, harmonica & vocal
Scarlet Rivera - violin
T-bone Burnett - guitar & piano
Steven Soles - guitar
Mick Ronson - guitar
Bobby Neuwirth - guitar & vocal
Roger McGuinn - guitar & vocal
David Mansfield - steel guitar, mandolin, violin & dobro
Rob Stoner - bass
Howie Wyeth - drums
Gary Burke - percussion

Joan Baez - vocal

April 14:
I'll Be Your Baby Tonight
Vincent Van Gogh
I Pity the Poor Immigrant
Blowin' in the Wind

April 15:
Just Like Tom Thumb's Blues
The Sun Is Shining
Lay Lady Lay
One More Cup of Coffee
It Takes a Lot to Laugh, It Takes a Train to Cry
Ballad of Hollis Brown
Hold Me in Your Arms
Mozambique
Idiot Wind
Shelter from the Storm
Isis
Rita May
I Threw It All Away
C. C. Rider Blues

April 17:
Stuck Inside of Mobile with the Memphis Blues Again
Going, Going, Gone
Just Like a Woman
Tomorrow Is a Long Time
Maggie's Farm
Seven Days
Sara
You Angel You

New songs being worked out for the tour include "Rita May", "Going, Going, Gone", "Tomorrow Is a Long Time", "Seven Days", "You Angel You", "Hollis Brown", "Stuck Inside of Mobile", and "I'll Be Your Baby Tonight" among others. "You Angel You", "Hollis Brown", and "Tomorrow Is a Long Time" were not performed at any of the shows. "Seven Days" is a pretty nice version of this rarely performed song, and an official live version appears on the first *Bootleg Series* box set.

The April 15 rehearsal is the best sounding, if a little on the distorted side. The other dates have a very distant sound to the vocals for the most part. What you mainly hear are bass and drums, and it's truly awful in most cases. The entire Clearwater Rehearsals are pretty grueling to listen to in their entirety, but a good compilation could be put together mainly featuring the one-off songs that didn't actually make it to the shows, as well as the best performances of the many run-throughs of the standard songs.

I would recommend the April 15 tape as the best of the lot, as there are some very interesting variations such as a sped-up version of "Isis" that sounds like no other version I have ever heard. Also, the renditions of "The Sun Is Shining" and "Hold Me in Your Arms" add some variety and sound pretty rocking! Too bad those songs were not performed at any of the shows.

LPs:
- **Clearwater**

CDs:
- **Going Going Guam**
- **The Days Before Hard Rain**

Ft. Collins Rehearsals
Colorado Hotel – May 23, 1976

Personnel:

Bob Dylan - guitar, harmonica & vocal
Scarlet Rivera - violin
T-bone Burnett - guitar & piano
Steven Soles - guitar
Mick Ronson - guitar
Bobby Neuwirth - guitar & vocal
Roger McGuinn - guitar & vocal
David Mansfield - steel guitar, mandolin, violin & dobro

Rob Stoner - bass
Howie Wyeth - drums
Gary Burke - percussion
Joan Baez - vocal

Just Like a Woman
Tangled Up in Blue

This tape consists of multiple run-throughs of both songs with very different arrangements. At a running time of approximately 60 minutes, it may be more versions of these two songs than are really needed, so I would recommend it more as a curiosity than as anything mandatory for one's collection.

CDs:
• **Going Going Guam**

The Tour Begins

Before the second half of the tour officially began on April 16, the Rolling Thunder Revue appeared at the second Hurricane Carter Benefit in Houston on January 25. As previously mentioned, the format of the Revue was pretty similar night after night. Most shows circulate either in complete or incomplete (Dylan-only) form. There are a few soundboard tapes that are worth checking out, but most are audience recordings.

Personnel for all shows:

Bob Dylan - guitar & vocal
Scarlet Rivera - violin
T-bone Burnett - guitar & piano
Steven Soles - guitar
Mick Ronson - guitar
Bobby Neuwirth - guitar & vocal
David Mansfield - steel guitar, mandolin, violin & dobro

Rob Stoner - bass
Howie Wyeth - drums
Gary Burke - percussion

Guest solo artists include:

Roger McGuinn
Kinky Friedman
Joan Baez (also duets with Bob)
Donna Weiss
Joni Mitchell

Recommended shows:

Night of the Hurricane II
Houston Astrodome, Houston TX – January 25, 1976

When I Paint My Masterpiece
Maggie's Farm
One Too Many Mornings
Romance in Durango
One Too Many Mornings
Isis
Positively 4th Street
It's All Over Now, Baby Blue
Oh, Sister
One More Cup of Coffee
Sara
Lay Lady Lay
Just Like a Woman
Hurricane
Ride 'Em Jewboy

This benefit concert for Hurricane Carter also included sets by Stevie Wonder and Isaac Hayes. The mono audience recording is the only one I know of, but be aware that, unless there is a better tape out there, it is a mediocre audience recording with a lot of chatter throughout. Ringo Starr and Joe Vitale also appear on drums. It actually seems more like a warm-up show for the actual tour, which makes it somewhat special and therefore recommended.

Of special note are the debuts of "Lay Lady Lay" (which I actually like here as opposed to the tedious version that appeared later in the tour), "Positively 4th Street", "One Too Many Mornings", and "Maggie's Farm". One odd moment occurs when Bob starts singing "I Threw It All Away" (which would have been a debut) but then switches quickly to "One Too Many Mornings".

Clearwater – April 22, 1976
Starlight Ballroom - Belleview Biltmore Hotel
Clearwater, Florida
Afternoon and evening shows

Both shows were filmed for a proposed TV special, but it was never released. Instead, the Fort Collins show was used for the NBC-TV special. A not very good bootleg copy of the proposed video exists and is worth seeking out. The audio copies available are incomplete PA tapes of varying quality. The evening show exists as a mediocre audience tape except for the songs that were included in the aborted TV special.

All in all, this would have made for a better TV show than what was ultimately shown. It is unknown why it was rejected, but perhaps someday it will show up as an official part of some future *Bootleg Series* release.

LPs:
- **Seven Days**

CDs:
- **Acoustic Thunder**
- **Like a Rolling Stone. The Hidden TV Shows**

New Orleans – May 3, 1976
The Warehouse – Evening show
New Orleans, Louisiana

Mostly complete soundboard tape available, with non-Dylan performances included, in acceptable quality. The Rolling Thunder Revue was best experienced in its entirety, and there are not many tapes available that include all or most of the performances from the entire Revue, and a soundboard tape is especially welcome. There are two tapes of this show circulating. One is, as noted, a relatively complete entire show and the other features just the Dylan portion.

LPs:
- **At the Warehouse**
- **Memphis Blues**
- **Together (Bob Dylan & Joan Baez)**

CDs:
- **Acoustic Thunder**
- **Creatures Void of Form**
- **Dared to Be Free**
- **Hold the Fort Lock up the Warehouse**
- **Live at the Warehouse**
- **Rolling Thunder EP**
- **Rolling Thunder Revue**

San Antonio – May 11, 1976
Municipal Auditorium
San Antonio, Texas

This partial soundboard features a nicely slowed down "Shelter from the Storm", as well as a nicely subdued "Romance in Durango". Bob is in especially good voice at this show, thus the recommendation. A complete audience tape of the Dylan set is in circulation as well. The audience portion has Dylan performing a rare "Spanish Is the Loving Tongue" as the opener.

CDs:
- **Blood and Thunder**
- **Discover Broken**

Fort Worth – May 16, 1976
Tarrant County Convention Center Arena
Fort Worth, Texas

The Dylan portion is a complete soundboard tape, but there is also an audience tape circulating that contains the entire Revue, not just the Dylan portion. Some tracks were included on the official *Hard Rain* album. This is one of the best performances from late in the tour. Highly recommended if you can find the complete audience tape.

LPs:
- **Together (Bob Dylan & Joan Baez)**

CDs:
- **Acoustic Thunder**
- **Hold the Fort for What it's Worth**
- **Hold the Fort Lock up the Warehouse**

Oklahoma City – May 18, 1976
State Fair Arena
Oklahoma City, Oklahoma

A complete audience recording (with a very noisy crowd) of the Dylan set is in circulation. Also, a partial soundboard tape exists with fourteen songs. These songs consist of:

Linda Lu (T-Bone Burnett)
Turn Turn Turn (Roger McGuinn)
Lover of the Bayou (Roger McGuinn)
Maggie's Farm
One Too Many Mornings (Incomplete)
Mozambique
Isis
I Pity the Poor Immigrant
Shelter from the Storm
Oh, Sister
You're Gonna Make Me Lonesome when You Go
Lay Lady Lay
I Want You
Going, Going, Gone

The soundboard portion of the show is well worth seeking out. The audience, not so much, unless you're looking to complete (as much as possible) the entire 1976 leg of the tour.

CDs:
- **Blood and Thunder**
- **Creatures Void of Form**
- **Hold the Fort Lock up the Warehouse**
- **The Tall Grass & the Ones I Love**

Fort Collins – May 23, 1976
Hughes Stadium, Colorado State University
Fort Collins, Colorado

Many songs from this show appear on the official *Hard Rain* album, as well as the NBC-TV special, therefore a good portion of this show is in circulation in excellent PA quality. There is also a complete audience tape from this above average show.

CDs:
- **Blood and Thunder**
- **Hold the Fort for What it's Worth**
- **Like a Rolling Stone. The Hidden TV Shows**
- **Complete Hard Rain**

Sign Language Sessions
Shangri-La Studios, Malibu – March-April 1976
With Eric Clapton

Spanish Is the Loving Tongue
The Water Is Wide
When the Ship Comes In
When I Paint My Masterpiece
Idiot Wind
Big River
Steppin' Out
Sign Language

This is part of a much longer tape that doesn't appear to include much, if any, Dylan involvement. The sessions for Eric Clapton's *No Reason to Cry* album were done with a large number of musicians, including all five members of The Band. The longer tape has jams with members of The Band and others, as well as outtakes from the sessions. One of the songs being recorded for the album was the previously unreleased Dylan song "Sign Language". According to the liner notes of *The Bootleg Series Volumes 1–3*: "Dylan dropped by and was just hanging out, living in a tent at the bottom of the garden. He would sneak into the studio to see what was going on. Dylan offered his new, unrecorded song 'Seven Days' to Clapton. Clapton passed on it, but Ron Wood took him up on the offer and released it on his third solo album *Gimme Some Neck*". The *No Reason to Cry* album does feature a duet with Dylan on "Sign Language", and this is the reason for the existence of this tape. The songs listed above appear, to these ears, to be the only songs of interest regarding Dylan's participation. One song, "Steppin' Out", sounds like Levon Helm on vocal. It's not entirely clear to me that Dylan is involved in that number, but it seems likely.

The sound is pretty good, being that it's a studio recording, and is interesting for the historic summit of two greats for one of Clapton's most successful albums, but musically this is not a necessary tape for any fan's collection. It's more of a curiosity than anything else.

CDs:
- **Acetates on the Tracks 3**
- **Happy Birthday Eric!**
- **Legend in His Time**
- **The Genuine Bootleg Series Vol. 2**
- **From Paradise to Shangri-La**

The Rundown Rehearsal Tapes
Rundown Studios, Santa Monica, California
December 1977 – February 1978

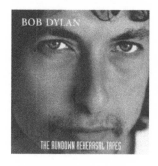

In preparation for Bob Dylan's first world tour since 1966, a series of rehearsals took place at Rundown Studios in Santa Monica from late 1977 until February 1978. The first session on December 26 is not in circulation, so the first available session is December 30.

December 30, 1977:

Personnel:

Bob Dylan - piano & vocal
David Mansfield - mandolin, guitar
Steven Soles - guitar
Alan Pasqua - organ
Rob Stoner - bass
Danny Seiwell - drums
Katey Sagal - background vocals
Frannie Eisenberg - background vocals

It's All Over Now, Baby Blue
Blowin' in the Wind
Maggie's Farm
Like a Rolling Stone
The Man in Me
To Ramona
Most Likely You Go Your Way (and I'll Go Mine)
Simple Twist of Fate
Leopard-Skin Pill-Box Hat
If Not for You
I Threw It All Away
I'll Be Your Baby Tonight

Early rehearsals show that the concept was closer to Rolling Thunder, using the same basic core band, except with more structure and the addition of backup singers and a keyboard player. Katey Sagal[1], by the way, is the same actress who became well known for playing Peg Bundy on *Married with Children* and later the voice of Leela on *Futurama*. In an interview for the Los Angeles Times in 2017, she has this to say about her involvement in these rehearsals:

> "I was like 19 or 20 years old. I shouldn't have been in the band in the first place. I'd already been in a band with one of these girls that was a friend of Bob's. She said Bob's looking for singers, come with me to the rehearsal. So I went. He just hired us, he didn't even listen to us. So before I knew it, I was in the band. I worked with him for like two months in rehearsal, then he fired all of us girls a week before the tour. But I still always consider it like I sang with Bob Dylan. I don't care if it was a week, you know what I mean?"

Alan Pasqua had previously been a member of the Tony Williams Lifetime and has an extensive background in jazz-rock fusion. In fact, I saw the Tony Williams Lifetime in a small club in San Francisco in 1976 (Keystone Korner) and was lucky to have sat about twenty feet away from the band, which also included the phenomenal Allan Holdsworth on guitar. I was surprised, and pleased, that Mr. Pasqua was a part of this band. Obviously, his versatility and talent was just what Bob needed. Most recently, he provided, at Bob's request, background piano for Bob's Nobel lecture. He is currently a professor at the University of Southern California.

As to how he became involved with Bob in the first place, he explains in an interview for the New York Times:

---

1 Dundas incorrectly spells her name "Katie Segal".

> "My first gig out of college was playing with Tony Williams, Miles Davis's drummer. While we were rehearsing at S.I.R. Studios in New York, I met a guy in the hallway named Rob Stoner, who was Bob's bass player. We started talking and became buds. Later Rob called, and said: 'I'm starting to put together a band for an upcoming tour. Why don't you come over and play for a little while, and I'll give Bob a tape.' That's how it all started."

This rehearsal tape shows that Bob was still in the process of auditioning band members. There was still no horn player or lead guitarist, and some musicians would be replaced. For instance, Denny Seiwell was part of the rehearsal band but would eventually be replaced by Ian Wallace. Denny Seiwell was previously in Paul McCartney's band Wings.

The quality is good to excellent.

Late December 1977 or Early January 1978:

Personnel:

Bob Dylan - vocal & guitar
Billy Cross - guitar
David Mansfield - mandolin, guitar
Steven Soles - guitar
Andy Stein - sax & violin
Alan Pasqua - organ
Rob Stoner - bass
Ian Wallace – drums
Katey Sagal - background vocals
Frannie Eisenberg - background vocals
Debi Dye - background vocals

You're Gonna Make Me Lonesome when You Go
Simple Twist of Fate
Going, Going, Gone

This is a fair to good stereo studio recording. By this time, more changes were being made to the band, which shows how serious Bob was in putting together exactly the right outfit for what was to be a completely new direction. For instance, he now has a horn player (Andy Stein). It is not entirely sure whether or not Ian Wallace is on drums at this point. Ian Wallace was previously a member of King Crimson. I find it interesting that Dylan would choose progressive-rock and fusion players to fill out his sound for this particular tour, even though they did not play in a Prog or Fusion style in this particular band. When asked how he got the gig, he replied:

> "I was doing some work in LA with a singer whose manager also managed Joan Baez. He knew Dylan was auditioning drummers and he recommended me. I auditioned, and got the gig."

January 1978:

Personnel:

Bob Dylan - vocal & guitar
Billy Cross - guitar
David Mansfield - mandolin, guitar
Steven Soles - guitar
Andy Stein - sax & violin
Alan Pasqua - organ
Rob Stoner - bass
Ian Wallace - drums
Katey Sagal - background vocals
Frannie Eisenberg - background vocals

Like a Rolling Stone
My Babe
Just Like a Woman
Blowin' in the Wind
I'll Be Your Baby Tonight
The Man in Me
You're a Big Girl Now
Don't Think Twice, It's All Right
I Threw It All Away
Love Minus Zero/No Limit
Maggie's Farm
Ballad of a Thin Man

Simple Twist of Fate
To Ramona
If You See Her, Say Hello
I Don't Believe You
Going, Going, Gone

The exact date is not known.

This is a good to excellent studio stereo recording. For this rehearsal, they are still working out the new "Like a Rolling Stone" arrangement, and they're not quite sure what it's going to be yet. "Blowin' in the Wind" is done in both a reggae version and a gospel version. With guitarist Billy Cross on board, the sound is really starting to come together.

January 27, 1978:

Personnel:

Bob Dylan - vocal & guitar
Billy Cross - guitar
David Mansfield - mandolin, guitar
Steven Soles - guitar
Andy Stein - sax & violin
Alan Pasqua - organ
Rob Stoner - bass
Ian Wallace - drums
Katey Sagal - background vocals
Frannie Eisenberg - background vocals

All I Really Want to Do
Absolutely Sweet Marie
Tomorrow Is a Long Time
Oh, Sister
The Times They Are A-Changin'
My Babe
Shelter from the Storm
Like a Rolling Stone
I Shall Be Released
All Along the Watchtower

This odd recording was done from the street outside of the rehearsal studio. It's poorly recorded and you can hear the tapers talking and fumbling with the portable recorder. Apparently the taper has a toddler with him and he tries to quiet the baby. He calls them the Golden Chords, but obviously he knows what he's listening to but doesn't want to tip his hand on the tape itself. Plausible deniability. This is an extremely poor recording, and it's really only worth seeking out for curiosity alone. If you manage to pick up the *Rundown Rehearsal Tapes* boot, you'll have this one as part of the package, so just make the most of it, I guess. Most of the tape is spent rehearsing "Tomorrow Is a Long Time".

January 27/30, 1978:

Personnel:

Bob Dylan - vocal & guitar
Billy Cross - guitar
David Mansfield - mandolin, guitar
Steven Soles - guitar
Andy Stein - sax & violin
Alan Pasqua - organ
Rob Stoner - bass
Ian Wallace - drums
Katey Sagal - background vocals
Frannie Eisenberg - background vocals

Shelter from the Storm
Don't Think Twice, It's All Right
Like a Rolling Stone
I Shall Be Released
All Along the Watchtower
I'll Be Your Baby Tonight
The Times They Are A-Changin'
If You See Her Say Hello
The Man in Me
I Don't Believe You
Tomorrow Is a Long Time

Blown Out on the Trail

As with the previous rehearsal tape, this is another street recording. Again, very poor quality. Unless it appears as part of some other collection of rehearsals, there's no reason to seek this out on its own.

January 30, 1978:

Personnel:

Bob Dylan - vocal & guitar
Billy Cross - guitar
David Mansfield - mandolin, guitar
Steven Soles - guitar
Steve Douglas - sax & violin
Alan Pasqua - organ
Rob Stoner - bass
Ian Wallace - drums
Bobbye Hall - percussion
Jo Ann Harris - background vocals
Helena Springs - background vocals
Debbie Dye - background vocals

I'll Be Your Baby Tonight
The Times They Are A-Changin'
If You See Her, Say Hello
The Man in Me
I Don't Believe You
Tomorrow Is a Long Time
You're a Big Girl Now
Knockin' on Heaven's Door
It's Alright, Ma (I'm Only Bleeding)
Forever Young

With Steve Douglas on saxophone, Bobbye Hall on percussion and Jo Ann Harris, Helena Springs and Carolyn Dennis on backing vocals, this would make it the definitive 1978 touring band, at least before Rob Stoner left and was replaced by Jerry Scheff.

Quality is good to excellent.

February 1, 1978:

Personnel:

Bob Dylan - vocal & guitar
Billy Cross - guitar
David Mansfield - mandolin, guitar
Steven Soles - guitar
Steve Douglas - sax & violin
Alan Pasqua - organ
Rob Stoner - bass
Ian Wallace - drums
Bobbye Hall - percussion
Jo Ann Harris - background vocals
Helena Springs - background vocals
Debbie Dye - background vocals

Repossession Blues
One of us Must Know (Sooner or Later)
Girl from the North Country

Quality is excellent stereo. "Repossession Blues" was only performed twice on the tour. Sounds like Dylan playing lead guitar on "One of us Must Know", which is a pretty good rearrangement of this rarely performed song.

April 28, 1978:

Personnel:

Bob Dylan - guitar & vocal
Billy Cross - guitar
Steven Soles - guitar & vocals
David Mansfield - violin & mandolin
Steve Douglas - saxophone
Alan Pasqua - keyboards
Jerry Scheff - bass
Ian Wallace - drums
Bobbye Hall - percussion
Helena Springs - background vocals
Jo Ann Harris - background vocals
Debbie Dye - background vocals

Blown Out on the Trail

We Better Talk This Over
Coming from the Heart
I Threw It All Away
Maggie's Farm
Ballad of a Thin Man
Simple Twist of Fate
To Ramona
If You See Her, Say Hello
I Don't Believe You

Good to excellent studio recording in stereo. After the Far East portion of the tour, these rehearsals took place for the upcoming LA shows in June. By this time, Rob Stoner had left the band and was replaced by Jerry Scheff, who used to play with Elvis Presley. Since this band was often referred to as the "Vegas band", the inclusion of Presley's ex-bass player seems fitting.

CDs:
- **The Rundown Rehearsal Tapes**
- **Darkness at the Break of Noon**
- **Moving Violation**
- **Rundown to Maggie**

1978 World Tour
February 17 – December 16, 1978

Bob Dylan - vocal & guitar
Billy Cross - lead guitar
Alan Pasqua - keyboards
Steven Soles - rhythm guitar, backup vocals
David Mansfield - violin & mandolin
Steve Douglas - horns
Rob Stoner - bass
Bobbye Hall - percussion
Ian Wallace - drums
Helena Springs - background vocals
Jo Ann Harris - background vocals
Debbie Dye - background vocals

This was the first time Dylan had done a world tour since 1966 — a twelve-year gap. It was an ambitious tour, certainly designed to keep the momentum going after the triumphs of last two US tours supporting three number one albums in a row. The tour began in February 20, starting in Japan, New Zealand, and Australia, and took a break while recording sessions for *Street Legal* took place in the spring of 1978. Then the tour continued in the summer starting in Los Angeles for a series of warm-up shows before continuing to Europe. In the fall, the tour came to the United States and finished up in Florida. There were a total of 115 shows.

The recording of *Street Legal* took place during a tumultuous time in his life. He had just gone through an acrimonious divorce and was struggling to finalize the film *Renaldo and Clara*. In addition, the sessions were interrupted by his reaction to the death of Elvis Presley, one of his early idols. Dylan was quoted as saying "I went over my whole life. I went over my whole childhood. I didn't talk to anyone for a week." As far as outtakes from the album, there are really none to speak of. For years there had been rumors of a tape of *"Street Legal* piano demos", but no such tape has ever turned up to my knowledge.

This tour was controversial in many ways. For one thing, longtime fans objected to the Neil Diamond/Las Vegas-Elvis style and all the radical re-arrangements of his classic songs. I, for one, appreciated that he was attempting something that he had never tried before: a professional big-band concert tour with tight arrangements and sophisticated musicality. It was basically his attempt at a real show-biz type of tour that he had never tried before, and after the rag-tag nature of the Rolling Thunder Revue, it came as a big shock. Many fans also labeled it the "Alimony Tour", because his marriage had just broken up and apparently he needed to recoup his losses. I won't get into all of that, other than to say that it could very well be that financial problems motivated this radical departure from the norm.

I've often heard other Dylan fans say that the later shows in Europe and the US were better than the earlier shows in the Far East, but I strongly disagree. I find those later shows to be too frantic and overblown, whereas the early shows, especially the first few in Japan, were more relaxed and assured. I would definitely give the edge to the shows at Budokan, and if the tour had ended there, I would have been perfectly happy with that outcome, but fortunately it kept going.

Recommended shows:

Tokyo – February 20, 1978
Nippon Budokan Hall
Tokyo, Japan

This is the first show of the 1978 World Tour. All of the Tokyo shows at Budokan are great, but this show is notable for the many debuts and energized performances of Bob and his big band. This is a mediocre to good audience tape, and my copy was slightly off-speed, but I would still recommend it simply because it is the first show of the tour and has energy that can't be denied. Features the only live version of "Something There Is About You" on the tour. It also has a great "Like a Rolling Stone" with the new revamped arrangement that I wish he had continued with in subsequent tours.

Two shows from Tokyo made up the official *Live at Budokan* album that was originally released only in Japan. These shows were February 28 and March 1. Due to popular demand, the double album was subsequently released in the US.

Brisbane – March 15, 1978
Festival Hall
Queensland, Australia

Aside from a few single songs here and there used as publishing demos, this is the only soundboard recording in circulation from the tour, but unfortunately it's only 90 minutes and not the complete show. It looks like the first song, which was almost certainly the instrumental "Hard Rain", is missing. Then it seems there is a big chunk missing in the middle where "Like a Rolling Stone" through "Just Like a Woman" would go. I am unaware of any complete audience tapes in circulation.

CDs:
- **Okay I Still Get Stoned**

Los Angeles – June 1, 1978
Universal Amphitheater
Los Angeles, California

First of a series of warm-up concerts for the second leg of the 1978 world tour. The only tape I've heard is an incomplete recording (only the second half after the intermission), but the sound is pretty incredible. I would like to find the rest of this show. The entire run of LA shows is worth seeking out, especially the June 2 show that appears on the vinyl bootleg *Life Sentence*. Sound quality-wise, the June 7 audience tape is particularly good, depending on which source tape you happen to find. I have heard several.

LPs:
- **Life Sentence**

Paris – July 3-8, 1978
Pavillon de Paris
Paris, France

All the Paris shows are well worth having. All are complete audience recordings in very good quality. These shows presented live debuts for several of the *Street Legal* songs. There are also a few soundchecks from these shows in circulation, but I have not heard them.

LPs:
- **Live in Paris '78**
- **Tangerine**

CDs:
- **My Back Pages**
- **Border Beneath the Sun**
- **Paris Is for Lovers**

Blackbushe – July 15, 1978
Blackbushe Aerodrome
Camberley, England

Known as The Picnic at Blackbushe Aerodrome, this was a one-day festival with Bob Dylan headlining in front of a crowd of 200,000, which is probably the biggest audience ever for Bob. Also on the bill were Eric Clapton, Joan Armatrading, Graham Parker and the Rumour, Greg Lake, and Merger. Eric Clapton guests on one song. Pretty good audience recording, although the crowd is noisy at times. This was the first time performing "Where Are You Tonight".

LPs:
- **By the Time We Got to Blackbushe**
- **Zim's Picnic**

CDs:
- **Blackbushe**
- **Picnic at Blackbushe**

Toronto – October 12, 1978
Maple Leaf Gardens
Toronto, Ontario, Canada

One of the best audience tapes from later in the tour. It's also a pretty energetic performance, even though I prefer the less energetic and more tightly focused early shows. Still, highly recommended for an example of what the band was sounding like midway through the tour. Dylan sings with great energy and enthusiasm throughout. At times it almost seems like he's narrating rather than singing, and he does this to great effect.

CDs:
- **I Was Young When I Left Home**

Hollywood – December 16, 1978
Hollywood Sportatorium
Hollywood, Florida

The last show of the tour is worth hearing just because of that, but also because of the debut of "Do Right to Me Baby", which prefigures the gospel period to come. The recording isn't too bad either.

The Gospel Tours
1979-1981

Sometime during the 1978 tour, Bob Dylan underwent a spiritual transformation that saw him embracing Christianity. I won't speculate too much on why this occurred, other than to note that Dylan was undoubtedly undergoing some turmoil in his life, not the least due to the collapse of his marriage.

According to legend, Dylan found Jesus in a Tucson hotel room. Supposedly, at the concert in San Diego a few days before, someone threw a cross up on the stage and he felt compelled to pick it up. He has been quoted as saying he felt "a presence in the room that couldn't have been anybody but Jesus. Jesus put his hand on me. It was a physical thing. I felt it. I felt it all over me. I felt my whole body tremble. The glory of the Lord knocked me down and picked me up." It was not long after that he joined the Vineyard Christian Fellowship, a religious cult group that also included

67

members of his current band. Thus began his three-year journey into born again Christianity.

As we have seen from *Trouble No More: The Bootleg Series Vol. 13,* the 1978 tour had Dylan performing some markedly different types of songs at some of the soundchecks and at some of the shows. These songs were of a distinctly religious nature and hinted at what was soon to come. What was to come took Jerry Wexler, producer of *Slow Train Coming,* completely by surprise, as it did guitarist Mark Knopfler, whom Dylan first became aware of when he heard "The Sultans of Swing" and saw Dire Straits at the Roxy in L.A. It was then that Dylan asked Knopfler to participate in his upcoming album, the nature of which Knopfler had no clue. The album sounded great, however, and is one of the best produced of his career. Jerry Wexler was hand picked by Dylan to produce the album, having been a big fan of the type of production Wexler had been involved in (Aretha Franklin, Wilson Pickett, Dusty Springfield) and wanted that type of sound for his next album. I admit to being a little skeptical at first, but when I heard the album (on a cassette tape while on tour with the band I was in at the time), it really struck home for me. It seems that Dylan had found a way to take gospel music and make it his own. The songs were, for the most part, very unusual and very interesting. As far as outtakes and unreleased songs, there is little out there. The few leftover songs from the sessions have been mostly officially released on various *Bootleg Series* albums and what little remain are not in circulation as of yet.

There is no doubt that the first gospel group was a great band. Since gospel music is often very close to blues, I hear this music as great blues with a gospel feel. It is not necessary to be a believer in Christ to appreciate the greatness of this music. I'm sure he did not approach it like this, but it almost seems as if the gospel format was a new way of expressing what he had been feeling all along – just another mythology to explore, like traditional folk music.

Fred Tackett sounds every bit as good as Eric Clapton or Mick Taylor or any other great blues guitarist Dylan has played with. Formerly with Little Feat, he got the call to do some rehearsals with Bob and the rest of what would become the members of the new gospel band he was putting together. The first gig Tackett had with Bob and the new band was for Saturday Night Live in October.

The rhythm section of Tim Drummond and Jim Keltner is one of the very best he has ever played with. Jim Keltner first played with Bob Dylan in 1971 when he was hired by producer Leon Russell to play on "Watching the River Flow" and "When I Paint My Masterpiece". He next played on the soundtrack for the film "Pat Garrett and Billy the Kid". That's him playing on "Knockin' on Heaven's Door". Tim Drummond, who passed away in 2015, had previously played with Neil Young on many albums, most especially on the *Harvest* album.

There is also no doubt that Dylan believed with all his heart that his newfound faith was true and pure, and it showed in the spirited and dynamic performances of the early part of the gospel years. His faith was so fervent that he couldn't keep himself from preaching the gospel at great length at many of this shows – a trend that would draw great ire from many in the crowd who had either not expected to hear what they were hearing or who knew what to expect and just wanted to show their displeasure. More on this later.

The first leg of the gospel tour era began in San Francisco with a series of shows at the Fox Warfield Theater from November 11 through November 16 of 1979. Shows continued in Southern California before moving to Arizona and New Mexico in December, where some of the most contentious shows occurred. After that, the tour continued in January of 1980 in the Pacific Northwest before moving to the Midwest and the Southern states in late January and February. The tour took a break while Dylan and the touring band took to the studio for sessions for the *Saved* album – most of the songs were already being performed prior to the

69

release of the 2nd gospel album, so anyone who had attended the live shows had already heard most of the material. Many who heard *Saved* after hearing the songs live were somewhat disappointed, but I think it's unfair to compare the two. To reject something because a different but similar item is better is poor criticism, in my opinion. The album is a truer representation of his gospel period than the previous album and he used the same studio and producers to capture what I think is a great live-in-the-studio version of a typical live show. To my knowledge there are no outtakes from these sessions in circulation.

April saw the tour move to Canada and the New England states before ending up in Ohio in May. When the gospel tour resumed in November 1980, things had changed. Dylan was now incorporating some of his classic older non-gospel songs in the set list, songs such as "Like a Rolling Stone", "Just Like a Woman", and "Blowin' in the Wind". As with the first gospel shows of 1979, he began this leg of the tour in San Francisco at the Fox Warfield Theater starting on November 9 and ending on November 22. Other shows followed in Southern California and Arizona before winding up in the Pacific Northwest with shows in Oregon and Washington.

Of special note is Dylan's appearance on *Saturday Night Live* at NBC Studios, Studio 8H, NYC October 20, 1979. This three-song performance is available officially on the Season 5 DVD set.

The first gospel band consisted of a core group of musicians:

Bob Dylan - vocal & guitar
Fred Tackett - guitar
Spooner Oldham - keyboards
Tim Drummond - bass
Terry Young - keyboards
Jim Keltner - drums

With the addition of:

Regina Mcrary - background vocals
Helena Springs - background vocals

70

Mona Lisa Young - background vocals

This lineup lasted from November 1979 through December 1979.

The second gospel band consisted of the core group plus:

Carolyn Dennis - background vocals
Regina Peeples - background vocals
Regina Havis - background vocals
Mona Lisa Young - background vocals

This lineup lasted from January 1980 through February 1980.

The third gospel band consisted of the core group plus:

Clydie King - background vocals
Gwen Evans - background vocals
Mary Elizabeth Bridges - background vocals
Regina McCrary - background vocals
Mona Lisa Young - background vocals

This lineup lasted from April 1980 through May 1980.

The fourth gospel band consisted of the core group except for the change of keyboard players from Spooner Oldham to Willie Smith. This band, also referred to as the "Musical Retrospective" band, spanned from November 1980 through December 1980. In addition, the backup singers were:

Clydie King - background vocals
Carolyn Dennis - background vocals
Regina McCrary - background vocals

The 1981 gospel band was basically the same as the "Musical Retrospective" band with the addition of:

Steve Ripley - guitar
Madelyn Quebec - background vocals

In October 1981 the band saw the addition of:

Al Kooper - keyboards

71

Arthur Rosato - drums (in addition to Jim Keltner)

This band spanned from October 1981 through November 1981, with the last show taking place in Lakeland, Florida, on November 21. By this time, though, the gospel content was much less than it had been when he started, and the addition of Al Kooper is likely one of the reasons for the gradual change.

Recommended shows:

San Francisco – November 1, 1979
Fox Warfield Theatre
San Francisco, California

Mediocre sound (audience), but great performance in front of a crowd that had never heard this music before. This was the first gospel show. Future shows would be more passionate, but this is recommended basically because it's the live debut of this new sound. All of the San Francisco shows are worth hearing, especially if you're a completist. Some of the songs from this set of shows appear on *The Bootleg Series Volume 13: Trouble No More*.

CDs:
- **New Found Faith**

Tempe – November 26, 1979
Gammage Center
Tempe, Arizona

This show is notorious for having one of the most hostile crowds Dylan played for in the early part of the 1979 tour. From the very beginning the crowd sounds angry, perhaps after hearing the pre-Dylan portion of the show with the gospel singers. Bob was especially talkative at this show, with much anger and frustration showing through. He tended to give long sermons by way of introduction to some of the songs, which no doubt fueled the anger in the crowd. Not everyone was hostile, however, and you can hear some positive feedback, but in general it was drowned out by a loud portion of the audience. Here is a sample of the sort of thing Bob was talking about in this show:

Well. What a rude bunch tonight, huh? You all know how to be real rude. You know about the spirit of the anti-Christ? Does anybody here know about that? Well, it's clear the anti-Christ is loose right now, let me give you an example. You know, I got a place out, ah, somebody stopped by my house and gave me this, uh, tape cassette. Some of these kind of people, you know, there's many false deceivers running around these days. There's only one gospel. The Bible says anybody who preaches anything other than that one gospel, let him be accursed. ["Rock-n-roll!"] Anyway, you know, this fellow stopped by my house one time and wanted to, so called, "turn me on" to a . . . well I'm not gonna mention his name, he's a certain guru. I don't want to mention his name right now, but ah, he, he has a place out there, near LA ["Malibu!"] And ah, he stopped by and he gave me this taped cassette to show me ... ["Rock-n-roll!"] ... You wanna rock-n-roll you can go down and rock-n-roll. You can go see Kiss and you rock-n-roll all your way down to the pit. Anyway, let me give you an example here. I'm gonna give you a real good example, I took a look, I dropped this tape cassette off with a friend of mine. [lots of heckling and others trying to shout the hecklers down] Turn the lights on in here. I want to see these people. Turn some lights on. Give them some light. Let them in the light. [applause] So anyway, this certain guru, you wanna hear about this guru? So anyhow, ["Rock-n-roll!" "Shut up!"] All right, so this guru, he made a film of himself. He had one of these big conventions. He does have a convention I think every so often like once a month, he'll go to a big city. ["Praise the lord with puke!" "Shut that guy up!" Applause] Now, so, I took a look at this tape, and sure enough he was having himself a big convention. He had, must have had five thousand to ten thousand people there. Eight thousand people. And what he was doing on the stage was, he was sitting on there with a lot of flowers and things. And he sure did look pretty though. He'd sit up there, you know like kind of like on a throne and you'd listen to him talk on the tape. And on the tape, he said, you know, what's life all about is life is to have fun. He said, "I'm gonna show you now how you all can have fun." And he had a big fire extinguisher there and he put colored water in this fire extinguisher, and he would spray it out on the people. And they all laughed and just had a good time. They took their clothes off. They were overjoyed to be sprayed by this man. [Booooo!] And a little while after that, he started talking about his philosophy. And he said that he was God -- he did say that. He said

73

that God's inside of him and he is God. And, you know, that those people could just think of themselves as God. I want to tell you this because there's many of these people walking around. They might not come right out and say they're God, but they're just waiting for the opportunity too. And there is only one God. And let me hear you say who that God is? [mixed shouts] Their God, he makes promises that he doesn't keep. There's only two kinds of people like the preacher says -- only two kinds of people. Color don't separate them, neither does their clothes ... [Rock-n-roll!] ... You still want to rock-n-roll? I'll tell you what the two kinds of people are. Don't matter how much money you got, there's only two kinds of people: There are saved people and there's lost people. [applause] Yeah. Now remember that I told you that. You may never see me again. I may not be through here again, you may not see me, sometime down the line you'll remember you heard it here. That Jesus is Lord. And every knee shall bow to him.

There was no encore, which was fairly unusual but understandable given the nature of this particular concert. All in all the crowd's anger seemed to fuel one of the most aggressive and interesting shows of the first gospel tour. The sound is pretty good for an audience recording.

Toronto – April 20, 1980
Massey Hall
Toronto, Ontario, Canada

This is a professionally recorded concert in excellent sound. Much of this has already been released on *The Bootleg Series Volume 13: Trouble No* More. Circulating in both audience (complete) and PA (incomplete). By this time the shows had become more assured and polished, and this show is very representative of the power of Dylan's vocals. Also, some new songs appeared, such as "Ain't Gonna Go to Hell for Anybody" and "Cover Down, Pray Through". Dylan spends some time giving long sermon-like introductions to his songs, but any hostile audience reaction that may have occurred is non-evident.

CDs:
- **The Born Again Music**
- **Gospeller**
- **Last Supper Serenade**
- **Rock Solid**
- **Solid Rock**

Hartford – May 8, 1980
Bushnell Memorial Hall
Hartfort, Connecticut

This is a great concert from when the show was still purely gospel. Bob is very talkative at this show. This is a pretty good representation of what the tour was like in 1980. If you only need one tape from this portion of the tour, this will do nicely. Pretty good audience tape too. Unfortunately, he does get into a rather embarrassing rap about homosexuality and San Francisco.

San Francisco – November 9, 1980
Fox Warfield Theatre
San Francisco, California

In 1980 Dylan added older songs back into his set list, therefore this tour has become known as the *Musical Retrospective Tour*. This show was the first, and while not necessarily the best sounding, it doesn't sound too bad at all. The circulating tapes that I have heard are complete, including the prelude featuring the gospel singers. The band, as usual, is great (one of his best) and the song selections are great. This tape features the live debuts of "Abraham, Martin and John" and "Let's Keep It Between Us".

This portion of the tour lasted from November 9 until December 4, where it wound up in Portland, Oregon. This series of shows was a good warm-up to the summer 1981 shows in support of *Shot of Love*.

As to why Dylan decided to return some of his pre-gospel songs to the set lists, that is up to speculation. It could be because of the backlash he was receiving from fans attending his concerts who were expecting to hear the classic hits, or it could be that ticket sales were suffering due to the exclusion of the older songs (although I am unaware of any evidence to support that). But most likely he just felt that it was time to reintroduce some of his best songs because they fit well in the mix. One thing you can tell for sure is that when he launches into "Like a Rolling Stone" for the first time since the 1978 tour, the crowd goes wild. Sure, it's a little rough, but it's an amazing moment and proof that Bob hadn't disappeared entirely into a fundamentalist haze.

San Francisco – November 15, 1980
Fox Warfield Theatre
San Francisco, California

Notable for the appearance of Mike Bloomfield, who plays on "Like a Rolling Stone" and "The Groom's Still Waiting at the Altar". I don't think I need to go into any detail about who Mike Bloomfield was or how important he was to the legacy of Bob Dylan. Unfortunately, Bloomfield died about three months later, so this would be the very last performance he did with Bob Dylan. Also of interest for the excellent sound quality, being a mostly complete soundboard recording.

CDs:
* **Farewell Bloomfield**

San Francisco – November 16, 1980
Fox Warfield Theatre
San Francisco, California

The complete show, including all the gospel singer songs. Of special note, Jerry Garcia guests on eleven songs. Bob had long been a true friend and admirer of Jerry Garcia, and there was even a rumor that he had recorded a session with the Grateful Dead in 1973, but no such recording has ever surfaced. This is their first public performance together. There is an excellent soundboard recording that contains most of the show and is absolutely essential.

LPs:
- **Live Adventures of Bob Dylan and Jerry Garcia**
- **Let's Keep It Between Us**

CDs:
- **Bob and Jerry**
- **Deep Blue Sea**
- **Duets**
- **Go Ahead with a Dead**
- **Keep in Touch with the Antichrist**
- **You Gotta Serve Somebody**

Seattle – November 30, 1980
Paramount Northwest Theatre
Seattle, Washington

This is an excellent complete show in very fine recording quality for a 1980 audience tape. Just a great representation of the Musical Retrospective tour of 1980. Very highly recommended.

CDs:
- **Rise Again**

Portland – December 3, 1980
Paramount Theater
Portland, Oregon

Another fine show in excellent sound. It's an audience recording, and like the Seattle show previously mentioned, it's a great recording of a typically great concert from the end of 1980. Definitely highly recommended.

LPs:
- **A.k.a. History volume 18-20**
- **Portland, Oregon**

CDs:
- **A Musical Retrospective**

Chicago – June 10, 1981
Hoffman Estates
Chicago, Illinois

After the 1980 shows, Bob took a break to record his next album: *Shot of Love*. In support of that album he did another gospel tour, only this time it not only featured older pre-gospel songs but also songs from the new album.

This show featured the first live performances of "Dead Man, Dead Man" and "Watered-Down Love". Again, not necessarily the best-sounding show from the tour, but certainly representative of where he was headed after his born again years.

London – June 28, 1981
Earls Court
London, England

The 1981 shows were better than both 1979 and 1980. The band was getting tighter and more adventurous. Fewer gospel songs were being played and Dylan was singing better than he ever had. This is a typically good audience recording from the string of London shows. I picked this one because it has long been a favorite of mine.

LPs:
- **Footsteps '81**
- **Gospel Rock and More**

Drammen – July 10, 1981
Drammenshallen
Drammen, Norway

A partial soundboard tape with excellent sound, which makes this a highly recommended recording if you can find it.

LPs:
- **Live in Oslo**

CDs:
- **In the Summertime**

78

Avignon – July 25, 1981
Palace des Sports
Avignon, France

Nearly complete soundboard recording of a show famous for an accident during the opening number where a member of the audience falls into electric cables and causes a power loss. The band improvises acoustically for about fifteen minutes while power is being restored. Tragically, two people were killed during this accident, but the show went on anyway. Aside from that, Bob just sings his heart out on this show.

CDs:
- **Avignon**
- **True Stories**

New Orleans – November 10, 1981
Saenger Performing Arts Center
New Orleans, Louisiana

For the US Fall tour, Dylan added Al Kooper and Arthur Rosato to the mix. In the case of Kooper, in particular, the sound of the band saw a slight return to the glory days of 1965, especially when hearing Kooper's classic organ figure in "Like a Rolling Stone". The first show took place in Milwaukee on October 16, 1981. This is an excellent soundboard recording, some tracks of which were officially released (see below) and was mixed by none other than Daniel Lanois. This is definitely one of the best sounding shows from the 1981 tour and a must. Two professional recordings in two subsequent nights lead me to believe Columbia may have been planning a live album. Of special note, this is the only known performance of "Thief on the Cross". Entire concert available on the excellent CD *Stadiums of the Damned*.

Officially released:

Heart of Mine [*Biograph*]
Thief on the Cross [*Trouble No More*]

79

Dead Man, Dead Man [cassette single and *Live 1961-2000*]

CDs:
- **Child's Balloon**
- **Stadiums of the Damned**
- **The Genuine Bootleg Series Vol. 1**

Houston – November 12, 1981
The Summit
Houston, Texas

This PA tape was recorded two nights after the November 10 New Orleans show, and as mentioned above, Columbia may have been intending to release a live album from this leg of the tour. Why that didn't happen, I can't really say, but this show, along with the New Orleans show described above, is very highly recommended.

LPs:
- **Cookie's Favorite**
- **In the Garden**
- **Standing Room Only**

CDs:
- **You Can't Kill an Idea**

Grammy Awards 1980
Shrine Auditorium
Los Angeles, California
February 27, 1980

The *Slow Train Coming* album was a huge success and it presented Bob Dylan with the first Grammy award of his career. He was nominated for Best Rock Male Vocal Performance for the song "Gotta Serve Somebody". His touring gospel band performed at the ceremony and he was presented with the award (by none other than Ted Nugent), much to his shock. "I didn't expect this," he said. "I want to thank the lord for it."

The performance is very good, with lots of spirit and enthusiasm, and helped to renew interest in Bob Dylan's music and gained some respect for his newfound religion. For a change, Bob was dressed in a tuxedo and seemed determined to impress, which he certainly did. The fact that Dylan, often characterized as someone who "could not sing" would get a Best Vocal award must have taken a lot of people by surprise. Suddenly he was well known as a great singer and not just a great songwriter. The crowd gave him a standing ovation and spotted in the audience were Johnny Cash, Kris Kristofferson, and Pat Boone, among others. Easily found on the Internet.

Shot of Love Sessions
March-April 1981

It's All Dangerous to Me
Well Water
My Oriental Home
Borrowed Time
Rockin' Boat
Movin' (on the Water)
I Want You to Know That I Love You
Yes Sir, No Sir (Hallelujah)
Is It Worth It?
Ah Ah Ah (aka High Away)
Almost Persuaded
Child to Me
Wind Blowin' on the Water
All the Way Down
More to This than Meets the Eye
Straw Hat
Walking on Eggs
Magic
Don't Ever Take Yourself Away
You Changed My Life
Mystery Train

The *Shot of Love* sessions started in March 1981 and continued through June. Most of what was recorded at the early sessions is not in general circulation. It's not until the sessions of March 25 and March 26 that we get anything that is commonly known – a take of "Angelina", which was used as a Special Rider demo. These sessions were produced by Jimmy Iovine, but Dylan wasn't satisfied with the results, so he went ahead with some sessions of his own, acting as producer, while looking for someone to replace Iovine. The results can be found on various bootlegs that contain variations of the above song titles. He found his next producer: Bumps Blackwell, who was best known for producing many hits for Little Richard. But due to health problems, Blackwell was unable to continue as Dylan's producer and so he brought in Chuck Plotkin, who was best known for his work with Bruce Springsteen, to continue the sessions.

Ultimately, the album would be complete, although lacking (as usual) some of the best songs recorded for the album. Of special interest is a rough mix tape in circulation that contains a different version of "Heart of Mine". At one time "Magic" was slated for inclusion on the album, but withdrawn at the last minute, along with "Angelina" and "Caribbean Wind" – both of which would have made the album even better than it was.

The songs recorded at the various sessions that are in circulation are a strange mixture of neo-gospel and contemporary pop, which pretty much describes the resulting *Shot of Love* album. There are some interesting songs and performances, but overall it represents a strange period in his career where he wasn't quite sure what to make of his newfound faith musically. If you are interested in this period, definitely check out *Between Saved and Shot* and the *Shot of Love Work Tapes and Outtakes* boots, if you can find them.

CDs:
- **Between Saved and Shot**
- **God Only Knows**
- **Shot of Love Work Tapes and Outtakes**

Peace Sunday Rally
Pasadena June 6, 1982

With God on Our Side
A Pirate Looks at Forty
Blowin' in the Wind

The Peace Sunday Rally was a six-hour anti-nuclear movement event that featured many artists throughout the day, including: Crosby Stills & Nash, Donovan, Stevie Wonder, Taj Mahal, Linda Ronstadt, Jackson Browne, Stevie Nicks, Tom Petty, and many others including Joan Baez and her special guest Bob Dylan. I don't know if the entire event was televised, but a portion was shown on *Entertainment Tonight* and raw footage of the entire event apparently exists somewhere. The Dylan/Baez portion is all we're interested in here, and the circulating tape, although taken from a soundboard recording, sounds muddy and lacking clarity. The performances themselves are not that great, but then I've never really liked the Dylan/Baez duets all that much. I don't think their voices blend that well. I think the casual fan could live without hearing this particular performance. For the completist, it is easily found on the Internet.

CDs:
- **Plugged, Unplugged and Jamming**

Lone Star Café 1983
New York City - February 16, 1983

Your Cheatin' Heart
Willie and the Hand Jive
Blues Stay Away from Me
Ain't No More Cane
Going Down

Rick Danko - guitar & vocal
Levon Helm - guitar & vocal
Bob Dylan - guitar & vocal

This is a guest appearance Bob made at a Rick Danko/Levon Helm show at the Lone Star Café. It's an audience tape that would have been pretty nice sounding if not for the loud and raucous crowd, but who could blame them? Three legends together singing covers of Hank Williams, Johnnie Otis, and some traditionals. Musically, this is extremely rough, but it must have been fun to be there. The songs mostly result from requests from the audience. Dylan can barely be heard, and he might as well not even be there. Is this recording a must? No way. For completists only.

CDs:
- **Lone Star Cafe**

Infidels Sessions
Studio A, Power Station, New York City
April-May 1983

Jokerman (alternate)
Clean-Cut Kid (alternate)
Sweetheart Like You (alternate)
License to Kill (alternate)
Neighborhood Bully (alternate)
Don't Fall Apart on Me Tonight (alternate)
I and I (alternate)
Union Sundown (alternate)
Dark Groove
Someone's Got a Hold of My Heart
Blind Willie McTell
Don't Fly Unless It's Safe
This Was My Love
Tell Me
Foot of Pride
Julius and Ethel
Death Is Not the End
Angel Flying Too Close to the Ground
Lord Protect My Child

In 1983 Bob Dylan launched yet another "comeback" and was looking for a new sound to follow up on the gospel direction he had been taking since 1979. The result was his most musically inspired album since *Slow Train Coming*, but this time without quite so much religion involved. Although many fans still see this as his first post-gospel album, I don't think that's quite right. I see it as the final four of the gospel era. Although not every song appeared to be religiously oriented, there were enough songs on the album to still give it the appearance of gospel: "Man of Peace" and "Jokerman" for instance. Even "Sweetheart Like You" and "License to Kill" seem steeped in a sort of new-age Christianity. Overall, though, there was a new political bent that we hadn't seen from him in ages. "Union Sundown" and "Neighborhood Bully", for instance. I think the most remarkable thing about the album was the group of musicians he chose for his new vision: Mick Taylor and Mark Knopfler on guitars; Alan Clark on keyboards; Sly Dunbar and Robbie Shakespeare as the rhythm section – the latter giving the sessions a sort of reggae feel while not being quite reggae.

The album was produced by both Mark Knopfler and Bob Dylan himself, but mostly the credit should go to Knopfler, who did a great job. Before Dylan decided on Knopfler, he had approached a number of other modern recording artists, such as Frank Zappa, David Bowie, and Elvis Costello. In fact, Zappa had quite a story to tell about this himself. From Michael Gray, in his book *Mother! The Frank Zappa Story*:

> "I get a lot of weird calls, and someone suddenly called up saying, 'This is Bob Dylan. I want to play you my new songs'." Zappa went on to say that he had never met Dylan before, but could see someone (via a video screen) in the cold, with an open shirt, and no coat. Gray quoted Zappa, telling Karl Dallas, that Dylan played eleven new songs on the piano, humming the lyrics. "I thought they were good songs. He seemed like a nice guy . Didn't look like it would be too hard to work with him."

For whatever reason, it never happened. Imagine what an album Frank Zappa could have produced for Dylan!

The unreleased songs sound great, being professional studio recordings, and some have been officially released – "Foot of Pride", "Someone's Got a Hold of My Heart", and "Blind Willie

McTell", for instance. But the greatest version of "Blind Willie McTell" has yet to be officially released. The bootlegs are worth seeking out just for that one track alone. The wealth of great leftover songs indicates that *Infidels* could have been a great double album. I especially like "Tell Me" and "This Was My Love". Most highly recommended of the bootleg CDs is *Rough Cuts*.

LPs:
- **Seven Days**
- **Toasted. The Australian Collection**
- **Don't Fall Apart on Me Tonight**
- **Down in the Flood**
- **Forty Miles from Nowhere**
- **Here I Am Again**
- **Idiot Wind**
- **Idiot Wind Again**
- **Outfidels**
- **Robert and Sara**

CDs:
- **Down in the Flood**
- **Friend to the Martyr (Outfidels)**
- **Infidels Sessions**
- **Rough Cuts**

Plugz Rehearsals
Malibu, California March 21, 1984
Bob Dylan's Home

Bob Dylan - vocal & guitar
Justin Poskin - guitar
Tony Marsico - bass
Charlie Quintana - drums
Clydie King (?) - backup vocal

Sometime in 1984, Dylan got together with the Plugz, a Latino punk band from Los Angeles that formed in 1977 and disbanded in 1984. It's likely that Dylan connected with the Plugz through Charlie Quintana's girlfriend who was then the secretary for Dylan's tour manager Gary Shafner. But, likely, Dylan also saw them play live and was impressed by their attitude and brash musicality. Charlie Quintana would later play in Bob's touring band for a brief period of time.

On this tape, which mostly consists of instrumental jams and run-throughs, Dylan cannot be heard for the most part. At one point someone tells Bob that there are some "cops coming", probably due to noise complaints.

Presumably these rehearsals are for the upcoming David Letterman Show appearance the next night of March 22 (see next entry for more details). It is also possible that he was intending to use the Plugz for his backup band on the upcoming tour. Maybe, but for whatever reason Bob chose to go with an entirely different, and more professional sounding band.

What can be heard here, though, is a sort of punk approach that he had never tried before, and it would have been pretty interesting if he had gone ahead with that. In some ways, it prefigures what he would do when he started the Never Ending Tour in 1988 when he toured with a small four-piece combo.

What we have here on this tape is pretty ragged and hard slogging, but somewhat rewarding nevertheless. I am unaware of any bootlegs containing this material other than "We Three" which appears on *The Genuine Bootleg Series Vol. 2.*

Among the easily identified songs are:

Jokerman
My Guy (instrumental)
We Three (My Echo, My Shadow and Me)
Lost on the River
Don't Start Me to Talkin'
Saved

Glen Dundas in *Tangled Up In Tapes* also lists the following songs:

Just One Look
Who Loves You More
Lonely Dreamer
Back in My Arms Again
Johnny Too Bad
A Woman Will Give You the Blues

David Letterman Show 1984
Rockefeller Center, New York City
March 22, 1984

Bob Dylan - vocal & guitar
Justin Poskin - guitar
Tony Marsico - bass
Charlie Quintana - drums

Rehearsal March 22, 1984:
I Once Knew a Man
Jokerman
License to Kill
Treat Her Right
My Guy

New York City, March 22, 1984:
Don't Start Me to Talkin'
License to Kill
Jokerman

Blown Out on the Trail

What has been characterized as a rehearsal is more likely a soundcheck. Raw footage of the entire rehearsal/soundcheck exists in fairly good quality, and can be found (as of this writing) on the Internet. The performances are ragged but interesting for what might have been, had he toured with this group of musicians instead of making it a one-off. As for the broadcast itself, I can still remember coming home from my swing shift and turning on, as I always did, the *Late Nite with David Letterman* show and, without warning, seeing that Bob Dylan was one of the guests, along with Liberace. That took me by surprise. What I heard was startling and very exciting. Most Dylan fans tend to agree that this was one of his very best TV performances of all time. I'm not aware of any official release, but it is available on several bootlegs.

CDs:
- **Magnetic Movements**
- **The Chair Is Not My Son**
- **The Complete Letterman Collection 1984-1993**
- **TV Guide**
- **Dirty Lies**

Tour Rehearsals 1984

Bob Dylan - vocal, guitar, harmonica
Mick Taylor - guitar
Ian McLagan - keyboards
Gregg Sutton - bass
Colin Allen - drums
Carlos Santana - guitar

Beverly Theatre May 23, 1984:

Maggie's Farm
All Along the Watchtower
Just Like a Woman
When You Gonna Wake Up
Shelter from the Storm
Watered-Down Love
Masters of War
Jokerman
Simple Twist of Fate
Man of Peace
I and I
It's All Over Now, Baby Blue
Ballad of a Thin Man
Heart of Mine
Highway 61 Revisited
I See You Around and Around
Leopard-Skin Pill-Box Hat
Unidentified Song
Always on My Mind
Every Grain of Sand
Girl from the North Country

Verona, Italy - Late May 1984:

Almost Done
Enough Is Enough
Dirty Lies
Why Do I Have to Choose?

To Each His Own
Jokerman
All Along the Watchtower
Just Like a Woman
Highway 61 Revisited
I and I
Girl from the North Country
Shelter from the Storm
License to Kill
Ballad of a Thin Man
When You Gonna Wake Up
To Ramona

When it came time to put together a band for the upcoming 1984 European tour, instead of going with the ragtag band of musicians he used for his appearance on the David Letterman show, he instead  asked Mick Taylor to put together a band that more closely resembled the sound of *Infidels*. He recruited ex-Small Faces keyboard player Ian McLagan along with Greg Sutton on bass and Colin Allen on drums. Mick Taylor had played with Colin Allen when both were members of John Mayall's Bluesbreakers. Carlos Santana doesn't appear on the Beverly Theatre rehearsal tape, but he does contribute quite a lot to the Verona rehearsal.

The Beverly Theatre rehearsal shows that Dylan was likely looking for a more muscular sound than usual. Using members of British rhythm and blues bands was certainly a new direction and the band sounds great here. It's about an hour and 20 minutes.

The Verona rehearsal tape is about an hour and a half and doesn't sound quite as good as the Beverly Theatre tape, which I was fortunate enough to find from someone who had a first generation copy right off of Colin Allen's personal reference tape. Still, the Verona rehearsal tape is essential, since it features Carlos Santana on most of the songs, many of which are just instrumentals. If you're a Santana fan (as I am), you will definitely want to hear this one.

LPs:
- **Dress Rehearsal**
- **Majestic Bells of Bolts**
- **Underdog Soldier – An Epitaph to America**

1984 European Tour
May 28 – June 8, 1984

Bob Dylan - vocal & guitar
Mick Taylor - guitar
Ian McLagan - keyboards
Greg Sutton - bass
Colin Allen - drums

The tour began in Verona, May 28 and continued throughout Europe before ending up at Slane Castle in Ireland on June 8. Mick Taylor is one of the best guitarists Dylan has ever played with, and his presence here helps Dylan to create a muscular British Blues sound that he had never attempted before. The closest he ever got was the *Highway 61 Revisited* sessions, but this band sounds nothing like that, nor anything like the band he toured with in 1966. It seems that the gospel period had officially come to an end because there was virtually nothing from the gospel era. Instead he focused on songs from all phases of his career, most notably the *Highway 61 Revisited* and *Blonde on Blonde* era. Of special note is a new version of "Tangled Up in Blue" with dramatically different lyrics.

100

Recommended shows:

Verona – May 28, 1984
Arena di Verona
Verona, Italy

The first show of the 1984 tour. I like to recommend first shows because they tend to be some of the most interesting, as it gives the listener a good overview of what's to be expected as the tour commences. The tape I have heard has mediocre sound, and a sometimes noisy crowd gets in the way. On this tour, Dylan gave Greg Sutton the spotlight (presumably to give himself a break) and he usually sang "I've Got to Use My Imagination", but on this premiere show he sings "Got My Mojo Working". Carlos Santana guests on "Blowin' in the Wind" and "Tombstone Blues". "Heart of Mine" has a false start and is pretty much a disaster. Later renditions would be better, but it's often the ragged moments that make an otherwise ordinary show worthy of attention.

LPs:
- **The Jokerman Plays in the Arena**

Rome – June 19, 1984
Roma Palaeur
Rome, Italy

This is one of the few soundboard recordings of an entire show, but it's not a very good mix. You can barely hear Mick Taylor's guitar, although it gets a little better towards the end. This is best heard on the Wanted Man CD boot *Oh the Streets of Rome*.

CDs:
- **Live at Palaeur**
- **Oh the Streets of Rome**
- **Rome '84 Revisited**

Barcelona – June 28, 1984
Minestadio del F.C. Barcelona
Barcelona, Spain

Probably the best of the 1984 European shows. Complete with about 45 minutes of encores! Very good audience recording.

LPs:
- **Barcelona**
- **Spanish Boot**

CDs:
- **From the Coast of Barcelona**

Paris – July 1, 1984
Parc de Sceaux
Paris, France

About half of this show is available as a PA recording. Guests include Hughes Aufray ("The Times They A-Changin'") and Van Morrison ("It's All Over Now, Baby Blue"). Excellent sound and performances.

CDs:
- **Les Temps Changent**
- **Over the Broken Glass**
- **Paris Par Excellence**

Slane – July 8, 1984
Slane Castle
Slane, Ireland

Some tracks appear on *Real Live*. A rather poor stereo audience recording exists for entire show, but many tracks (nearly 90 minutes) are in circulation as PA recordings. The PA tape I have heard sounds pretty muddy, but a decent mix overall. Of special note is the appearance of Van Morrison on "It's All Over Now, Baby Blue" and "Tupelo Honey". Bono also sings on "Leopard-Skin Pill-Box Hat" and "Blowin' in the Wind" (your mileage may vary on that). Carlos Santana also plays guitar on the final seven songs.

Empire Burlesque Sessions

1984 was the year that Dylan appeared to have lost the plot. After the comeback success of *Infidels* and the successful European tour promoting the album, he headed into a long period of wandering aimlessly through the wilderness. As always, there were high spots to counter-balance the lows of the era, but for a good five years or so he appeared to  be lost. Thus began a series of recording sessions for the next album.

The sessions were produced by Bob himself, but later Arthur Baker, best known for his work with New Order, was called in to put his finishing touches on the album. Those "finishing touches" were a great subject of controversy for many fans. *Empire Burlesque* was poorly received, both by critics and fans, most often being criticized for its sterile '80s production style and excessive overdubs, not to mention the seemingly low quality of the songs themselves. It seemed obvious to me at the time that he was going for a mainstream pop sound that did not quite fit, and I was initially disappointed with the album. Only the last song, "Dark Eyes", seemed to hint that there might have been more to the album than appeared at first listen. Was there actually a really good album in there somewhere, underneath all the polish and flash? When bootlegs started coming out featuring what appeared to be raw tracks before overdubs and studio tricks by Arthur Baker were added, fans suspected that the album had been sabotaged by Bob himself. As usual, he left off the best song! "New Danville Girl" would appear under a different title ("Brownsville Girl") on the next album, but the original recording from the *Empire Burlesque* sessions was, in my opinion, much better.

Listening to the album again recently, I have slightly changed my mind about many things. First of all, I have never minded '80s production styles. I may be more tolerant of it than most people, for whatever reason, but the thing that struck me most was that the music – overproduced as it may be – is pretty good and the songs are generally great. I think what sinks the album most of all is the voice. I can't help but think that if he had managed to employ his *Blood on the Tracks* voice it would have been pretty damn great. As it is, in the mid '80s Dylan was affecting a nasal sound that tended to distract from the overall compositions.

Here is a breakdown of the sessions that produced the mostly unreleased tracks. There were other sessions, but I won't note them here because they mostly resulted in the officially released takes that appear on the album and are not of much interest for the purpose of this book. There still remain many songs that are not in circulation.

Oceanway Studios, Los Angeles
November 1984

In the Summertime
Freedom for the Stallion
Instrumental # 1
Help Me Make It Through the Night
Instrumental # 2
Instrumental # 3
Instrumental # 4
Instrumental # 5

Sound is fair to good studio recording, mostly involving instrumentals where Bob's participation is unconfirmed. This session was the first of many for what was to become the *Empire Burslesque* album, although none of these songs made the album. None are original compositions, which is unlike the eventual album, which featured all originals. Perhaps this was more of a run-through to see which musicians and musical approach he would eventually decide upon. Note that "In the Summertime" is not the original from *Shot of Love*, but is instead the Mungo Jerry hit. The backing musicians are unknown.

July 1984 – March 1985

New Danville Girl
Straight A's in Love
Go Away Little Boy
The Very Thought of You
Who Loves You More
Waiting to Get Beat
Driftin' Too Far from Shore

As previously mentioned, "New Danville Girl" is the undisputed highlight of the *Empire Burlesque* sessions, and it's a real puzzle why he would leave this one off and instead redo the basic tracks with a new vocal, new lyrics, and different backing instruments. The other songs are equally arresting: "Straight A's in Love" and "Go Away Little Boy" are well worth hearing, and of course "Driftin' Too Far from Shore" would eventually wind up on *Knocked out Loaded*. More on that later.

CDs:
- **Important Words**
- **Ashes & Dust**

Live Aid 1985

Philadelphia July 13, 1985

On July 13, 1985, a huge benefit event took place in two locations (Wembley Stadium in London and John F. Kennedy Stadium in Philadelphia) and was broadcast worldwide. The purpose of the benefit was to raise funds for Ethiopian famine relief. The featured artists at the all-day pair of concerts included such superstars as Mick Jagger with Tina Turner; Queen; David Bowie; U2; Joan Baez; Elvis Costello; B. B. King; Sting; The Beach Boys; The Who; Elton John; Tom Petty; Neil Young; Led Zeppelin; Pink Floyd; and many others, including, of course, Bob Dylan, along with Keith Richards and Ron Wood, in one of the most highly anticipated closing sets of the entire event. First, there were some rehearsals for the event.

Live Aid Rehearsals

July 12, 1985
Ron Wood's Home

Bob Dylan - guitar, vocal, harmonica
Keith Richards - guitar
Ron Wood - guitar

Ballad of Hollis Brown
Girl from the North Country
Trouble

Blowin' in the Wind
Careless Ethiopians
Little Maggie
When the Ship Comes In
Dark Eyes

Recorded at Ron Wood's house, this rehearsal features Bob Dylan, Keith Richards, and Ron Wood running through some potential songs to perform at the event. Of special interest is a run-through of "Dark Eyes". It would have been nice if that had actually been performed, but it was not to be. There is a lot of interesting conversation throughout the circulating tape, including some commentary about Mick Taylor. All seemed to agree that he had some problems with following through on commitments, probably due to drug-related issues, but all agreed, of course, that he was one hell of a guitar player.

The sound is pretty good and is highly recommended for a glimpse of what the performance might have been like if they had put just a little more effort into it. This is best represented on the CD boot *Voices of Freedom*.

Live Aid Concert – July 13 1985
John F. Kennedy Stadium
Philadelphia, Pennsylvania

Bob Dylan - guitar, vocal, harmonica
Keith Richards - guitar
Ron Wood - guitar

Ballad of Hollis Brown
When the Ship Comes In
Blowin' in the Wind

Given the exalted timeslot given over to Bob and company, it was a huge disappointment to fans and non-fans alike that the performance was so ragged. It was quickly panned and added to Dylan's sinking reputation in the mid '80s. The concert portion itself is readily available in numerous places, and so shouldn't be too hard to find. At one point in the performance, Bob broke a string and Ron Wood quickly gave his guitar over to him. During the performance Dylan said "I hope that some of the money ... maybe they can just take a little bit of it, maybe ... one or two million, maybe ... and use it, say, to pay the mortgages on some of the farms and, the farmers here, owe to the banks. ... " This comment was the inspiration for the Farm Aid concert event which took place in September of 1985.

LPs:
- **The Day the World Rocked**
- **Live Aid. The Global Juke Box Vol. 2**
- **Live Aid. A Short Shame Story**
- **Now's the Time for Your Tears**

CDs:
- **Special Night-Special Guests**
- **Voices of Freedom**

20/20 Interview
Bob Dylan's home in Malibu, California
September 19, 1985

A lucid interview for the ABC television TV show *20-20* with Bob Brown. A lot of time is spent with the interviewer asking questions about the recording process, about protest songs, and politics. Bob is polite in his answers but reserved. The purpose of the interview was, no doubt, to publicize the upcoming Farm Aid concert (see next section). Part of the interview was broadcast on *20-20* and the entire interview itself exists as raw TV footage. I am unaware of any LPs or CDs that contain this interview.

Farm Aid 1985

Bob Dylan - vocal & guitar, keyboards, harmonica
Tom Petty - guitar &vocals
Mike Campbell - guitar
Benmont Tench - keyboards
Howie Epstein - bass
Stan Lynch - drums
Debra Byrd - backing vocals
Queen Esther Marrow - backing vocals
Madelyn Quebec - backing vocals
Elisecia Wright - backing vocals

As previously mentioned, one of Bob Dylan's comments at Live
Aid sparked the Farm Aid event organized by Willie Nelson, Neil
Young, and John Mellencamp. The purpose of the event was to
raise money for struggling farmers in the United States. In addition
to Dylan, Nelson, Young, and Mellencamp there was also the
Beach Boys; Johnny Cash; Arlo Guthrie; B. B. King; Lou Reed;

Billy Joel and numerous others. Most important for Dylan fans was the appearance of Tom Petty and the Heartbreakers, for it was at this concert that Bob Dylan and Tom Petty got together for the first time.

From an interview with Tom Petty in *American Songwriter* published 2012:

> When Bob played in Live Aid he went on right before the finale with only acoustic guitars, and people were tuning up behind him, and it was pretty disastrous. So when Willie Nelson invited him to perform in Farm Aid, Bob didn't want to play acoustic, he wanted to have an electric band behind him. So we went down and rehearsed. We rehearsed a lot. Played a lot of songs. He loved the Heartbreakers. It was quick and easy. You could just throw something out, and the Heartbreakers were good at grabbing it and going for it. We rehearsed and learned more songs than we needed.

This concert was the beginning of a long friendship and all-too-brief collaboration between the two artists.

Farm Aid Rehearsals

Los Angeles, California
September 1985

I Shall Be Released
Gotta Serve Somebody
Across the Borderline
Señor (Tales of Yankee Power)
Trouble
Clean Cut Kid
I'll Remember You
That Lucky Old Sun
Maggie's Farm
In the Garden
Shot of Love

111

Sing Me Back Home
Union Sundown
Come Together
This Was My Love
Lonesome Town
License to Kill
Lenny Bruce
Rocky Road Blues
Never Gonna Be the Same Again
Baby Please Stop Crying
Shake
Tight Connection to My Heart
Dead Man, Dead Man
Heart of Mine
Red Cadillac & a Black Mustache
Under the Boardwalk
Seeing the Real You at Last
Emotionally Yours
I and I
Under the Boardwalk/Save the Last Dance for Me
Heart of Mine (Instrumental)
Trust Yourself

This excellent sounding recording was the first of several rehearsals and contains a lot of songs and song fragments. Available on the Rattlesnake CD boot *The 1985 Rehearsal Tape.*

Los Angeles, California
September 19, 1985

What'd I Say
Baby What You Want Me to Do
Shake
I'll Remember You
Then He Kissed Me
Forever Young
Trust Yourself
Louie, Louie

That Lucky Old Sun

Exists as raw TV footage readily found on the Internet. No official release. The Heartbreakers were really good at doing this sort of thing – 1960s rock and roll classics. Apparently, this is what Dylan was interested in as well, which is why they got along so well. Basically they were just trying out grooves and having a good time. They also did a bunch of instrumental jams. Were they really planning on playing "Louie, Louie" at the show? Who knows? Mediocre sound overall.

Memorial Stadium
University Of Illinois
Champaign, Illinois
September 21, 1985

Shake
Trust Yourself
That Lucky Old Sun
Maggie's Farm
I Like It Like That

A fairly poor sounding tape from the "audience", and the final rehearsal before the show. It's really more of a soundcheck than an actual rehearsal.

Farm Aid Concert – September 22, 1985

Memorial Stadium
University Of Illinois
Champaign, Illinois

Clean Cut Kid
Shake
I'll Remember You
Trust Yourself
That Lucky Old Sun

Maggie's Farm

Even though it was broadcast live on TNN (The Nashville Network) among others, the entire performance is most commonly circulating as a mediocre audience tape. Only four songs were broadcast: "Shake", "I'll Remember You", "Trust Yourself", and "Maggie's Farm". The performances were very good and a far cry from the Live Aid debacle. The tight Heartbreakers were the best band he had played with since The Band, and it seemed like a pretty natural combination. Willie Nelson joins the band for the final song.

LPs:
- **Now and Then**
- **Now's the Time for Your Tears**
- **Then & Now / Farm Aid**

Knocked out Loaded Sessions
Cherokee Studio
Los Angeles, October 31 1985

Baby Coming Back from the Dead
Nothing Here Worth Dying For
Won't Go Back 'Til They Call Me Back Again
Let Me Come, Baby
Bring It on Home to Me
I'm Ready for Love
26 Storeys High
You Can Have Her
My Sweet Baby (Around & Around)
Find Me
Right Hand Road Blues
That's All

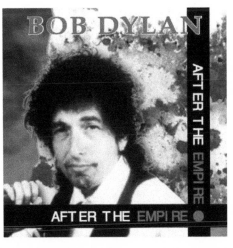

These songs, recorded after *Empire Burlesque* but unreleased for whatever reason, were likely intended for the follow-up album which would eventually become *Knocked out Loaded*. The sound is excellent studio quality and there are some great performances and the songs show some potential. It's a shame that none of the songs from this session found official release. Backing musicians and singers unknown for the most part.

Knocked Out Loaded is one of Dylan's most controversial albums, and is widely considered to be one of the very worst of his career. Bob himself produced it. About the only thing it has going for itself is "Brownsville Girl", which, as previously mentioned, is a reworked version of "New Danville Girl", which was recorded for and left off of Empire Burlesque. Even though the original tracks were modified, with new lyrics and vocals, it is still a great track and is certainly one of the best things he did in that decade. Still, the original version is much better. Al Kooper, who participated in sessions for the album, said: "There was enough stuff cut...to put out a great album, but I don't think we'll ever hear 'em..."

CDs:
- **After the Empire**

Martin Luther King Day 1986
John F. Kennedy Performing Arts Center
Washington D.C.
Opera House

Bob Dylan - vocal & guitar
Madelyn Quebec - backup vocals
Peggi Blu - backup vocals
Queen Esther Marrow - backup vocals
The Quincy Jones Orchestra

I Shall Be Released
Blowin' in the Wind

117

An all-star celebration honoring Martin Luther King Jr., on what has come to be known as "Martin Luther King Day", hosted by Stevie Wonder. Other guests included Joan Baez, Diana Ross, Neil Diamond and many others. "I Shall Be Released" features some drastically different lyrics: "I see my light come shining. I don't need a doctor or a priest". Peter, Paul, & Mary join Stevie Wonder and Bob Dylan on "Blowin' in the Wind". This is a fair audience recording that might make a nice filler to some other tape, but otherwise it's typical of the all-star events that Bob was participating in during the '80s. Not essential, but nice to have as filler.

CDs:
- **Be My Guest**
- **Hard to Find Volume 3**
- **Hard to Find Volume 4**
- **Precious Memories Volume 5**
- **You Don't Know Me**

True Confessions Tour
February – August 1986

Bob Dylan - vocal & guitar
Tom Petty - guitar
Mike Campbell - guitar
Benmont Tench - keyboards
Howie Epstein - bass
Stan Lynch - drums
The Queens of Rhythm (backup vocals):
Debra Byrd, Queen Esther Marrow, Madelyn Quebec, Elisecia Wright

After the successful collaboration between Bob Dylan and Tom Petty and the Heartbreakers at Farm Aid, it seemed only natural that they would go out on a tour together. The Heartbreakers seemed like the perfect backing band, and indeed they were. I would especially like to single out Benmont Tench for his excellent keyboard work, as well as Mike Campbell on lead guitar. The tour, dubbed "True Confessions", began in New Zealand, February 5, and continued through March 10, in Tokyo, Japan.

From an interview with Tom Petty in *American Songwriter* published 2012:

> So we backed him up at Farm Aid and it went really well. And then afterwards in the trailer, Bob came back and said, "Hey, what would you think of doing a tour? I've got a tour of Australia I want to do, and what would you guys think of doing that?" And we'd all been huge Dylan fans, and we were very intrigued by the idea of playing with Bob. So off we went. And that went on for two years. We'd do part of it and

119

then more would get added on, and then more would get added on. We really did the world with Bob Dylan.

The only fault I may find with the tour was the relatively stiff nature of some of the arrangements, especially compared to the loose nature of the Rolling Thunder Revue and the upcoming "Never Ending Tour" which commenced in 1988. Still, there were some outstanding shows.

Recommended shows:

Sydney – February 24-25, 1986
Entertainment Centre
Sydney, New South Wales, Australia

Excellent PA tape for both shows, portions of which were officially released on the commercial VHS *Hard to Handle*, which was also broadcast on HBO. In addition, portions were also broadcast on the radio on the SUPERSTAR CONCERT SERIES by Westwood One. The entire February 24 show is available in complete PA quality on the boot *True Confessions for Carol*, which also includes the Tom Petty sets. The February 25 show is available in a complete audience tape with only the released songs available in PA quality. Bob is very talkative throughout.

LPs:
* **Inspiration**
* **Live Down Under**

CDs:
* **Duelling Banjos**
* **Live USA**
* **Lonesome Town**
* **Precious Memories**
* **True Confessions**
* **True Confessions for Carol**

Akron – July 2, 1986
Rubber Bowl
Akron, Ohio

Notable for an appearance with the Grateful Dead during their encores. Bob opened for the Grateful Dead at this show and the three numbers Bob appeared on are in very good soundboard quality. The songs are "Little Red Rooster", "Don't Think Twice", and "It's All Over Now, Baby Blue", but Bob does not sing on the first of these.

LPs:
• **Joint Adventures**

Buffalo – July 4, 1986
Rich Stadium
Buffalo, New York

Some of this was broadcast by satellite for Farm Aid 2. Most of the show is available in very good PA quality.

LPs:
• **Fourth of July Song and Dance**

CDs:
• **Rich for Poor**

Washington DC – July 7, 1986
RFK Stadium
Washington, District Of Columbia

A fairly decent soundboard recording, probably thanks to the Grateful Dead fans who routinely provided excellent line recordings. Later, Bob would join the Dead during their encores.

Saratoga Springs – July 13, 1986
Saratoga Performing Arts Center
Saratoga Springs, New York

Excellent soundboard recording. Circulating tape includes the Tom Petty sets.

LPs:

- **Saratoga**

CDs:
- **There Is a Place of Broken Dreams**

Mountain View – August 5, 1986
Shoreline Amphitheatre
Mountain View, California

From my old stomping grounds, this is yet another soundboard tape, and well worth seeking out. Of special note are guests Al Kooper and John Lee Hooker. Also features the Tom Petty sets. Probably about as good as it gets.

CDs:
- **There Is a Place of Broken Dreams**

Park Royal Hotel Jam 1986
Park Royal Hotel
Wellington, New Zealand
February 6, 1986

Supposedly Bob Dylan with Tom Petty and the Heartbreakers goofing off in a hotel lounge in Wellington. What it actually seems to be is just Benmont Tench at the piano playing a bunch of tunes, including the theme for *Route 66* and a bunch of other familiar things of that nature. Occasionally you can hear someone attempting to sing, for instance on a brief version of "Save the Last Dance for Me". Reportedly, Stevie Nicks is one of the participants, but I don't know how anyone could really tell. Just a horrible audience recording. Not really worth seeking out unless you're a completist.

Dire Straits Concert Appearance 1986
Melbourne Sports and Entertainment Centre
Melbourne, Victoria, Australia
February 19, 1986

All Along the Watchtower
Leopard-Skin Pill-Box Hat
License to Kill
Knockin' on Heaven's Door

Bob makes an appearance at a Dire Straits concert in Melbourne, Australia. Mediocre audience tape, but the performances are pretty good, especially hearing Mark Knopfler's lead guitar. It's a shame that he didn't get to play more live dates with Bob.

No known bootlegs, but it shouldn't be too hard to find on the Internet.

Bob Fass Radio Show 1986
Topanga Park, California
May 21, 1986

A phone interview with Bob, broadcast live by WBAI, New York City, on May 21 of 1986 in a Bob Dylan birthday program. This is a very dull interview, but Bob Fass tries really hard to get him to open up. A lot of the problem seems to stem from Bob's inability to hear the questions. He often has to ask for repeats and misunderstands an awful lot of the questions. He doesn't really seem to want to be doing the phone-in in the first place, so it's hard to know why this interview even exists. It's quite a contrast from the 1966 Bob Fass show where Dylan was wildly funny and surrealistic. That's probably what Fass was expecting, but the 1986 Bob was much different from the 1966 Bob. It's actually very painful to listen to because of all the awkward moments. Bob is just not very talkative and the interviewers just don't know what to say to get him to be more talkative. It's sad, really, and it shows just how much Bob Dylan had changed from 1966 to 1986.

The entire tape is about 40 minutes long.

Amnesty International Benefit 1986
Los Angeles June 6, 1986

Bob Dylan - vocal & guitar
Tom Petty - guitar
Mike Campbell - guitar
Benmont Tench - keyboards
Howie Epstein - bass
Philip Lyn Jones - congas
Stan Lynch - drums

Band of the Hand
License to Kill
Shake a Hand

One of six concerts for Amnesty International under the name "Conspiracy of Hope" in June 1986. The purpose of the tour was to raise awareness of human rights and of Amnesty's work on its 25th anniversary. Bob Dylan, along with Tom Petty and the Heartbreakers, gave a performance on June 6. This performance is available as raw TV footage, but it appears the only circulating tape is a noisy but listenable audience tape. I, myself, have not seen the raw footage, so I can't comment on that. The performances themselves are pretty good and worth seeking out, if only to add as filler to another Dylan/Petty concert tape.

Grateful Dead Jam 1986
RFK Stadium
Washington, District of Columbia
July 7, 1986

Satisfaction
It's All Over Now, Baby Blue
Desolation Row

Bob Dylan opened the show for the Grateful Dead and he appears during the Dead's encore section playing guitar on "Satisfaction" but does not sing. A typically ragged Grateful Dead performance and only worth hearing if you are a fan of the group. It's also from a good soundboard tape, so the sound quality makes it a little more worthwhile.

127

Providence Hotel Jam 1986
Marriott Hotel
Providence, Rhode Island
July 10, 1986

Bob Dylan - guitar & vocal
Etta James - vocal
Shuggie Otis - guitar
Jack McDuff - organ
Richard Reid - bass
Paul Humphrey - drums

You Win Again
I'm a King Bee/Stormy Monday
Let the Good Times Roll
Earth Angel
Goodnight, Sweetheart, Goodnight

Jam session in the lounge of the Marriott Hotel with Etta James' band. Seems to be an audience recording. A bit ragged, but not bad overall. Bob had previously recorded "You Win Again" with The Band during the Basement Tapes sessions. Recommended for the fun they all seem to be having.

LPs:
- **Charlie's Choice**
- **Dreams**
- **What's Happening Here?**
- **Zim Zim Zabob**

Chabad Telethon 1986
Mountain View, California
Shoreline Amphitheatre
August 5, 1986

Thank God

Filmed during a soundcheck at the Shoreline Amphitheatre
in Mountain View with Tom Petty and the Heartbreakers and
broadcast in September 1986 for The Lubavitcher's Chabad
Telethon. Bob did several appearances for Chabad, the others being
in 1989 and another in 1991. It seems to have been a favorite
charity of his. The performance is pretty good and appears to be the
only time he ever performed it in public. Because the performance
was televised, it can easily be found on the Internet, but I am
unaware of any boot CDs that contain the performance, although
I'm told that it appears on a Tom Petty boot.

Hearts of Fire Sessions
Townhouse Studio
London, England
August 27-28, 1986

Bob Dylan - vocal & guitar
Eric Clapton - guitar
Ron Wood - bass
Kip Winger - bass
Beau Hill - keyboards
Henry Spinetti - drums

The Usual
Ride This Train
Had a Dream About You, Baby
Old Five and Dimer
To Fall in Love with You
Night After Night
A Couple More Years

For the first time since 1973, Bob Dylan decided to make another film as an actor, or he was talked into it. Not sure which. I'm not sure that *Renaldo and Clara* counts, but if you want to consider that to be a fictional film with Bob as an actor, fine. After the harsh reviews for that film, it's surprising that he would choose to make another, and especially one that he had no real creative input into, other than the soundtrack. The film *Hearts of Fire* had some pretty good credentials going for it: screenplay by Joe Eszterhas (*Basic Instinct, Jagged Edge, Flashdance*); directed by Richard Marquand (*Return of the Jedi, Jagged Edge, Eye of the Needle*); a cast that included Rupert Everett, Julian Glover, and the unknown Fiona Flanagan. In fact, this turned out to be Richard Marquand's final film before his death in 1987. The film was poorly received and Bob himself has since disowned it. I have to confess that I have

130

never actually seen it myself, although copies are not that hard to find. What we're more interested in here is the soundtrack.

Sessions for the soundtrack to the film *Hearts of Fire* took place in August 1986 and an excellent studio quality tape is in circulation that runs approximately 70 minutes and features many outtakes of songs that appeared on the soundtrack album and some that didn't. The tape features lots of different variations of "Had a Dream About You, Baby", and the song is certainly not worth the effort put into it, in spite of the stellar supporting players such as Eric Clapton and Ron Wood. Still, "Old Five and Dimer" has a pretty good vocal and "The Usual" (written by John Hiatt) and "A Couple More Years" are well worth hearing. Overall, another missed opportunity for the floundering Bob Dylan of the 1980s.

The Silver Wilburys
The Palamino Club
Los Angeles, California
February 19, 1987

Bob Dylan - vocal & guitar
Taj Mahal - vocal & harmonica
George Harrison - guitar and vocal
John Fogerty - guitar and vocal
Jesse Ed Davis - guitar
Wayne Henderson - keyboards
Ray Fitzpatrick - bass
Kester Smith - drums

Matchbox
Gone Gone Gone
Lucille
I'm Your Crosscut Saw
Bacon Fat
Knock on Wood
In the Midnight Hour
Honey Don't
Blue Suede Shoes
Watching the River Flow
Proud Mary
Johnny B Goode
Willie and the Hand Jive
Hey, Bo Diddley
Peggy Sue
Dizzy Miss Lizzy
Twist and Shout

Bob makes a surprise guest appearance at a Taj Mahal show at the
Palamino Club in Los Angeles along with friends George Harrison

132

and John Fogerty. The appearance was jokingly referred to as the Silver Wilburys because of the Dylan/Harrison connection. Fairly decent soundboard recording but there's really not much Dylan content. "Watching the River Flow" is attempted, but in a very shambolic fashion. Dylan can't be heard. John Fogerty does a great "Knock on Wood", "In the Midnight Hour", and "Proud Mary" among others. George Harrison sings "Matchbox", "Honey Don't", and "Blue Suede Shoes", among others. Essential? Not really, but fun to listen to at least once.

CDs:
- **Live! The Silver Wilburys**
- **Golden Wilburys**

George Gershwin Celebration
Brooklyn Academy of Music
New York City, March 11 1987

Soon

Dylan makes another one-off appearance, this time at the George Gershwin Celebration Concert on March 11, 1987. It was later broadcast by ZDF-TV, West Germany, 7 July 1987. The performance is solo acoustic. The video is easily found on the Internet and the audio (excellent stereo PA) is found on several bootlegs. A very odd performance, but there you have it.

CDs:
- **Hard to Find Vol 5**
- **If My Thought Dreams Could Be Seen**
- **Spanish Is the Loving Tongue (Plugged, Unplugged and Jamming Vol. 2)**
- **You Don't Know Me**

Down in the Groove Sessions
Los Angeles, April 1987

Just when I Needed You Most
Important Words
Willie and the Hand Jive
Twist and Shout

Excellent studio recordings from sessions for the album that would eventually be called *Down in the Groove*. For whatever reason Dylan decided to do an album of covers, supposedly originally to be called *Self Portrait Volume 2*, but the final album was not all covers and contained a mixture of (poor) originals and (occasionally interesting) covers. Some odd numbers here, such as "Twist and Shout" and "Willie and the Hand Jive", but none of the songs made it to the eventual album.

Again, he ostensibly produced the album himself, and the results demonstrated more than ever that he needed a good producer. He was about to find one with the subsequent album, but for this go 'round, the results were poor. Perhaps the album was only slightly better received than his previous one, but not by much. The outtakes that we do have available sure don't show a lot of promise, but the songs would have fit perfectly fine in the context of the album.

One thing he managed to do was collaborate with the Grateful Dead for the first time on record. The song "Silvio", co-written with Grateful Dead lyricist Robert Hunter, remained a staple of his live shows for many years to come. The Grateful Dead play on the track. Hunter also co-wrote the awful song "Ugliest Girl in the World".

135

The outtakes contained on the CD *Important Words* are worth listening to at least once. Maybe twice.

CDs:
- **Important Words**

U2 Concert Appearance 1987
Sports Arena, Los Angeles
April 30, 1987

I Shall Be Released
Knockin' on Heaven's Door

Guest appearance at the U2 concert in Los Angeles. If you're a fan of Bono, you will love this. If not, what can I say? All in all, it's some ragged performances and Bob can't really be heard that well. What they had in common at the time was producer Daniel Lanois, who was yet to produce *Oh Mercy*. Fairly good audience recording.

CDs:
- **Cover of Love**
- **Covering 'Em**
- **Helter Skelter in Times Square**
- **New Horizon**
- **Spanish Is the Loving Tongue (Plugged, Unplugged and Jamming Vol. 2)**
- **The Total Thing**
- **Unforgettable Duets**

Grateful Dead Rehearsals 1987
Club Front
San Rafael, June 1987

Bob Dylan - vocal & guitar
Jerry Garcia - vocal & guitar
Bob Weir - vocal & guitar
Phil Lesh - bass
Brent Mydland - keyboards
Bill Kreutzman - drums
Mickey Hart - drums

The French Girl
Blues Stay Away from Me
John Hardy
I'm So Lonesome I Could Cry
The Times They Are A-Changin'
When I Paint My Masterpiece
Man of Peace
I'll Be Your Baby Tonight
The Ballad of Ira Hayes
I Want You
Ballad of a Thin Man
Stuck Inside of Mobile with the Memphis Blues Again
Dead Man, Dead Man
Queen Jane Approximately
In the Summertime
Union Sundown
It's All Over Now, Baby Blue
Joey
If Not for You
Slow Train
Tomorrow Is a Long Time
Walkin' Down the Line
Gotta Serve Somebody
Gonna Change My Way of Thinking
Maggie's Farm
Chimes of Freedom
All I Really Want to Do

John Brown
Heart of Mine
Rolling in My Sweet Baby's Arms
The Ballad of Frankie Lee and Judas Priest
Don't Keep Me Waiting Too Long
Stealin'
Oh Boy
Tangled Up in Blue
Simple Twist of Fate
The Boy in the Bubble
Pledging My Time
Senor (Tales of Yankee Power)
The Wicked Messenger
Watching the River Flow
Under Your Spell
I'm Free
They Killed Him
All Along the Watchtower
Folsom Prison Blues
Hideaway/C C Rider

Dylan finally realized a long-time desire to collaborate with one of his favorite bands: the Grateful Dead. Jerry Garcia had been a Dylan admirer for a long time, but Dylan's reciprocal appreciation was not very well known, though for a long time there had been rumors of a Dylan/Dead session taking place as far back as 1973. No such session has ever turned up,  and so it was chalked up for many years to someone's fevered imagination. But it turns out that Dylan and the Dead really had a connection, and somehow it all came together in 1987. Supposedly, but who really knows, Dylan wanted to join the band on a permanent basis. Considering that a few years later Dylan became a "member" of the Traveling Wilburys, it doesn't seem too outrageous to think that he really wanted to be a part of a group and not always the leader and driving force. The collaboration with the Dead almost gave him that opportunity.

These tapes are all in excellent sound, being semi-professionally recorded during the rehearsals for the upcoming Dylan/Dead tour. The Dead have a really good feel for Dylan's music and the combination was much more successful than I would have imagined. There are a lot of great songs that were tried but never performed during the tour, for instance "The Ballad of Ira Hayes", "John Hardy", and "The French Girl". All in all, these rehearsals are very highly recommended.

LPs:
- **Studio Sessions – Volume One**
- **Sundown on the Union**

CDs:
- **The Complete Rehearsals (So Far)**
- **The French Girl**
- **San Rafael Rehearsals**

Grateful Dead Tour
July 1987

The tour consisted of six shows from July 4 through July 26:

July 4 – Foxboro, Massachusetts
July 10 – Philadelphia, Pennsylvania
July 12 – East Rutherford, New Jersey
July 19 – Eugene, Oregon
July 24 – Oakland, California
July 26 – Anaheim, California

Recommended shows: All of them, really. They were all recorded from the soundboard, as was typical for Grateful Dead shows, so they all exist in excellent quality, and all performances are typically very good.

The entire tour was apparently recorded by Columbia for the live album *Dylan & the Dead*. The album was a bit of a disappointment considering all the great material from which they had to choose, but still, the album was a nice souvenir of this very short tour.

LPs:
- **Dylan, Dead, Live up to Legend**
- **Together We're Strong**
- **Mad Mystic Hammering**
- **Bridget's Album (Bob Dylan & the Grateful Dead)**
- **Triumph**

CDs:
- **Bob Dylan with the Grateful Dead**
- **A Dream Came True**
- **Foxboro**
- **Knockin' on Foxboro's Door**
- **Orbiting Uvula**
- **Unreleased Live Album**
- **Ballad of Bob & Jerry**
- **Men of Peace**
- **I'll Be Your Robert Today**
- **Dylan Plays Dead**
- **Bob Dylan with the Grateful Dead Live Vol 2**
- **In the Heart of Oregon**

Temples in Flames Tour
September – October 1987

For the first time ever, Dylan did a tour of the Middle East. Instead of teaming with the Grateful Dead again he chose to use Tom Petty & the Heartbreakers. Roger McGuinn was a special guest on the tour. I am unaware of any PA or soundboard recordings from this tour, only audience tapes.

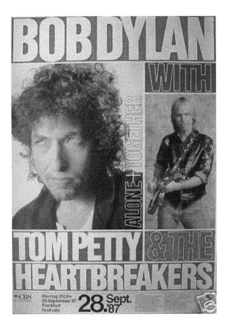

It was at one of the shows on this tour (Locarno, Switzerland) that Dylan claims he had an epiphany that led to the Never Ending Tour in 1988. In a Newsweek interview published in 1997:

> "I'd kind of reached the end of the line. Whatever I'd started out to do, it wasn't that. I was going to pack it in." Onstage, he couldn't do his old songs. "You know, like how do I sing this? It just sounds funny." He goes into an all-too-convincing imitation of panic: "I–I can't remember what it means, does it mean–is it just a bunch of words? Maybe it's like what all these people say, just a bunch of surrealistic nonsense." When The Grateful Dead took him on tour in 1987, Jerry Garcia urged him to try again. "He'd say, "Come on, man, you know, this is the way it goes, let's play it, it goes like this.' And I'd say, "Man, he's right, you know? How's he there and I can't get there?' And I had to go through a lot of red tape in my mind to get back there."

Then, in October 1987, playing Locarno, Switzerland, with Tom Petty's band and the female singers he now says he used to hide behind, Dylan had his breakthrough. It was an outdoor show–he remembers the fog and the wind–and as he stepped to the mike, a line came into his head. "It's almost like I heard it as a voice. It wasn't like it was even me thinking it. I'm determined to stand, whether God will deliver me or not. And all of a sudden everything just exploded. It exploded every which way. And I noticed that all the people out there–I was used to them looking at the girl singers, they were good-looking girls, you know? And like I say, I had them up there so I wouldn't feel so bad. But when that happened, nobody was looking at the girls anymore. They were looking at the main mike. After that is when I sort of knew: I've got to go out and play these songs. That's just what I must do." He's been at it ever since.

Could be an exaggeration, but in any event something crucial happened to change his way of approaching live performing, and it would show after this tour when he would embark on the Never Ending Tour.

Recommended shows:

Tel-Aviv – September 5, 1987
Hayarkon Park
Tel-Aviv, Israel

First show of the tour. The audience tape I have heard is not too bad. The band sounds great and Bob's singing is energetic and he seems pretty focused. A good start to the tour.

CDs:
- **Over Europe**
- **Visit to Israel**

Torino – September 13, 1987
Palasport
Torino, Italy

Good audience tape. Well balanced mix of instruments and voices. Good song selection. Highly recommended.

LPs:
- **Over Europe**
- **Shot of Bob**
- **Temples in Flames: 1987 Tour Anthology**
- **Torino 1987**

Stockholm – September 26, 1987
Johanneshovs Isstadion
Stockholm, Sweden

This is one of the better audience tapes from the tour, and the performances are typically good for this tour.

LPs:
- **Live in Scandinavia 1987**

Locarno – October 5, 1987
Piazza Grande
Locarno, Switzerland

Notable for being the show that is referenced in the Newsweek interview. The "epiphany show" if you will. Mediocre audience tape, however.

CDs:
- **The Final Night and More**

Brussels – October 8, 1987
Vorst Nationaal
Brussels, Belgium

Another good audience tape. One notable thing about this tour was the great variety of opening numbers. This time he opens with "Desolation Row", which seems like an unusual choice, but it works.

CDs:
- **Flashing for the Refugees**

London – October 15, 1987
Wembley Arena
London, England

One of the few shows featuring the complete Roger McGuinn and Tom Petty sets as well.

London – October 17, 1987
Wembley Arena
London, England

Last show of the tour. George Harrison guests on "Go Down Moses". Another good audience recording.

LPs:
*   **Wild Cathedral Evening**

G.E. Smith Audition Tape
New York City, New York
Studio Instrumental Rentals
November 22, 1987

Bob Dylan - guitar
G. E. Smith - guitar and back-up vocal
Randy Jackson - bass
Steve Jordan - drums

Dancing in the Dark
Six Days on the Road
Prince of Darkness
Suzie Q
You're a Big Girl Now
All I Really Want to Do
Leopard-Skin Pill-Box Hat
Dead Man, Dead Man
Everybody's Movin'
Easy
Trail of the Buffalo
Heart of Mine
Joey
I'll Be Your Baby Tonight
Folsom Prison Blues
Shelter from the Storm

As previously mentioned, Dylan explained that he had experienced an epiphany during the 1987 "Temples in Flames" tour with Tom Petty and the Heartbreakers, whereby he rediscovered whatever it was that was missing from his performance art. What this amounts to in my mind is that he had finally come to the end of his long artistic drought and was about to experience a renaissance of sorts and finally renew the flame that had been seemingly extinguished after his conversion to Christianity in 1978. Even though that conversion resulted in some magnificent recorded music and performances, it seems that he was unable to sustain that energy throughout the following decade and was lost in the wilderness, searching this way and that for a direction forward. The epiphany, whether real or metaphorical, was the beginning of a new era. And now he was about to embark on what many fans consider to be his greatest period of live performance: the G. E. Smith era. There are a great many fans who despise G. E. Smith, both as a guitarist and as a stage presence, but there is no doubt in my mind that he was the perfect choice for a musical director in this new stage of Bob's career. The sound that Dylan was going for, apparently, was a minimalist approach somewhat similar to what might have occurred had he toured with the Plugz back in 1984. However, G. E.'s professionalism, and the professionalism of his cohorts, was something new. This new tight four-piece band (including Bob) could take on any song from Bob's catalog and transform it into something new and exciting each and every night. Thus, a new variety entered into the nightly repertoire that made each and every show of the Never Ending Tour an event to behold.

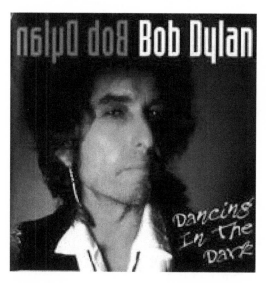

This, then, is the G. E. Smith audition tape, although it is actually being described in most places as a rehearsal. Either way, it appears to be the earliest tape we have of the Dylan/Smith combination. Randy Jackson and Steve Jordan are said to be the rhythm section. The sound is pretty good, but the performances are understandably a bit ragged. After all, it is Dylan playing (allegedly) for the very first time with this particular team of musicians.

Not only does G. E. sing on a few tracks, but he is also credited with playing accordion on "Trail of the Buffalo". Ultimately, neither Steve Jordan nor Randy Jackson appeared in any of the Never Ending Tour bands.

CDs:
- **Dancing in the Dark**

Rock and Roll Hall of Fame Jam 1988
New York City
January 20 1988

Twist and Shout
All Along the Watchtower
I Saw Her Standing There
Stand by Me
Stop! In the Name of Love
Whole Lotta Shakin' Goin' On
Hound Dog
Hi Ho Silver
Barbara Ann
Born on the Bayou
Like a Rolling Stone
(I Can't Get No) Satisfaction

In 1988 Bob Dylan became eligible for induction into the Rock and Roll Hall of Fame, established and located in Cleveland, Ohio. The purpose of the Hall of Fame is to honor the musicians, bands, producers and others that have had some major impact on the music industry, particularly (but not limited to) Rock and Roll. Bob was inducted the first year he was eligible, which would be twenty-five years after the release of his first album. As usual with Hall of Fame induction ceremonies, there was a musical presentation, and this consisted of other Hall of Fame inductees as well as various guests and presenters. The musical presentation in this case was a jam that included George Harrison, Mick Jagger, Brian Wilson, Billy Joel, Bruce Springsteen, John Fogerty, Ben E. King, and many others. The circulating recording includes Bruce Springsteen's speech about Bob Dylan and Bob Dylan's acceptance speech. It's in circulation as a sixty-minute mono PA recording. As of this writing video of the induction and jam session is available on the Internet.

I know of no bootlegs containing this material, but some of it has been officially released on *The Best of the Rock and Roll Hall of Fame* from *Time Life*.

Traveling Wilburys Outtakes 1988
May 1988

Bob Dylan - guitar, keyboards & vocals
George Harrison - guitar & vocals
Roy Orbison - guitar & vocals
Tom Petty - bass, guitar & vocals
Jeff Lynne - guitar, synthesizer, keyboards & vocals
Ray Cooper - percussion
Jim Keltner - drums
Ian Wallace - tom toms

Like a Ship
Maxine

In 1988 Bob Dylan did something that he had never done before. He recorded an album as part of a band and not as a solo artist. There had certainly been collaborations between himself and a band that stood apart as significant recording and performing artists (The Band, the Grateful Dead, Tom Petty and the Heartbreakers), but never as an equal member of a band that featured multiple singers and songwriters. And in this case, the other members of the new band were already superstars, making this a true supergroup in the best sense of the word. Jeff Lynne was probably the least known of the group members, but he had already been in two highly successful groups: The Move and The Electric Light Orchestra, and was an active and successful producer. The

Wilburys never actually performed in person, only releasing two studio albums, the second of which did not include Roy Orbison, who had passed away prior to the sessions.

The idea for the group first came up during sessions for George Harrison's *Cloud Nine* album. Harrison needed a bonus track for a single and got together with the other members, including producer Jeff Lynne, who was also producing Tom Petty's solo album as well as an album for Roy Orbison. After recording the track, they all decided it was so good they should record an entire album. And so, The Traveling Wilburys were formed. The album was a great success and helped to boost Dylan's comeback even further.

Only two outtakes exist from the sessions for the first album: "Like a Ship" and "Maxine". I am unaware of any bootleg LPs or CDs that contain these tracks, but they are in circulation among collectors. Dylan sings lead on "Like a Ship" and "Maxine" is sung by George Harrison. Both tracks are well worth seeking out.

By the way, the name Wilburys is an inside joke based on the expression "we'll bury it in the mix". Originally George Harrison wanted to call the band The Trembling Wilburys.

Lone Star Café 1988
New York City, May 29 1988

The Weight
Nadine

Bob Dylan makes a guest appearance at a Levon Helm show at the Lone Star Café In New York City. He proves that he doesn't really know the lyrics to "The Weight". Just enough to get by. Much better is "Nadine", with a fairly good Dylan vocal. All in all, an enjoyable tape easily found (as of this writing) on the Internet. Very good audience tape.

No known bootlegs.

Never Ending Tour 1988

In 1988, Dylan had just released the album *Down in the Groove* to rather poor critical and fan reception. Naturally, he went out on tour to promote the new album. This turned out to be a very different live experience from what most fans had come to expect. Rather than use an existing group like the Heartbreakers or the Grateful Dead or The Band, he put together a small group of musicians – the smallest he had ever played with – utilizing a very different sound. As previously noted in the section covering the 1987 "Temples in Flames" tour, Dylan had reputedly undergone a transformation of some kind that caused him to re-evaluate the way he had been performing. The result, apparently, was what was to become known as "The Never Ending Tour". There is some truth to this, in that he took very short breaks between trips out and about, which gave the impression of almost constant touring, but also used the same group of musicians for long periods of time. The changes to the band personnel were minimal and mostly served to bring in a different guitarist or drummer but playing basically the same set of tunes in the same basic style. It should be noted that Dylan plays a lot of electric guitar on this tour, often to great effect as G. E. is soloing.

The core band in the beginning was:

Bob Dylan - vocal, harmonica, guitar
G. E. Smith - guitar
Kenny Aaronson - bass
Christopher Parker - drums

G. E. Smith was with the band for three years. Kenny Aaronson lasted two years. Christopher Parker outlasted both of them at four years. Even with the band changes, the basic sound remained the same and certainly showed some great improvements along the way, especially in the years not covered by this book – 1997 to present. Personnel changes will be covered in subsequent sections on the Never Ending Tour.

All of the 1988 shows are pretty good. They also have the advantage of being recorded very well, seeing as portable recording equipment had become very sophisticated by that time, so there are some excellent sounding audience tapes in addition to a nice selection of soundboard tapes that made for some very nice CD bootlegs at the beginning of that era. Tapes were still the preferred medium for trading the music, but soon home CD-R units would become readily available to anyone who could afford it.

Even though he was ostensibly touring to promote *Down in the Groove*, he actually played very few songs from that album. The one song that remained a mainstay for years was "Silvio". He also did "Driftin' Too Far from Shore", "Rank Strangers to Me", and "Had a Dream About You, Baby", but that's about it.

The most recommended shows:

Concord – June 7, 1988
Concord Pavilion
Concord, California

First show of the never ending tour. 1988 shows were also known as "Interstate 88 Tour". Neil Young plays with the band through most of the show, but he sits out the acoustic set. Imagine how shocked the audience must have been to hear the band kick into "Subterranean Homesick Blues" – a live debut. Who would have imagined such a high energy live rendition of this song as an opener? It pretty much set the pace for the rest of the show, and indeed for the rest of the tour, at least the next few years. The recording itself is one of the best audience recordings I've heard from this tour. Some people have mistaken this for a soundboard, but it isn't. This is an absolute must.

Berkeley – June 10, 1988
Greek Theatre
University Of California
Berkeley, California

Neil Young sits in again, but only on the second half of the show after the acoustic set. Sound is once again an excellent audience recording. Some surprises here, such as "Joey".

Mountain View – June 11, 1988
Shoreline Amphitheatre
Mountain View, California

This was the 3rd and final show with Neil Young sitting in, again only on the 2nd half of the concert. Another excellent audience recording well worth hearing. This show can be found on the Wanted Man CD *Driftin' Too Far from the Shore*.

Wantagh – June 30, 1988
Jones Beach Theater
Jones Beach State Park
Wantagh, New York

This is a fantastic soundboard recording of an excellent show. This appears to be the first soundboard from 1988 that became available to collectors. This recording can be found on the bootleg CD *Blown Out on the Trail* (sound familiar?)

Mansfield – July 2, 1988
Great Woods Performing Arts Center
Mansfield, Massachusetts

Another great soundboard recording from 1988. Features a live debut of "Pretty Peggy-O", and it's a good one. There is also an excellent audience recording in circulation. Some may even prefer that to the soundboard.

Montréal – July 1988
Forum de Montréal
Montréal, Quebec, Canada

157

Good audience recording. Notable for the first performance of Leonard Cohen's "Hallelujah".

Los Angeles – August 3, 1988
Greek Theatre
Los Angeles, California

A real favorite of mine. A strong show with some truly incredible performances. Best "Like a Rolling Stone" I've heard from the Never Ending Tour. Pretty good audience recording.

George – August 20, 1988
Champs de Brionne Music Theater
George, Washington

Another outstanding show. Could very well be the best of 1988. If not, it certainly comes close. Brutal "Absolutely Sweet Marie" and "Masters of War". Excellent sounding audience recording. If you only need one 1988 show, this is the one.

Bristol, Connecticut
Lake Compounce Festival Park
September 4, 1988

Again, a great soundboard recording; also a typically great show. Available on the CD bootleg *Wanted Man*, but with wrong information. It gives the date as August 4, 1988 and credits Marshall Crenshaw on bass.

Upper Darby – October 13, 1988
The Tower Theatre
Upper Darby, Pennsylvania

Longest 1988 show - close to two hours. Acting as a sort of warm-up for the extended NYC shows of a few days later, Dylan and band are in peak form. Good audience recording.

New York City – October 16-19, 1988
Radio City Music Hall
New York City, New York

All of the New York shows from the 1988 run of the NET are great. Of special note is the 19th, which is a soundboard and most famously available on the boot *Stuck Inside of New York*. I think I actually prefer the audience tapes from the 17th and 18th.

Bridge School Benefit 1988
Oakland Coliseum
Oakland, California
December 4, 1988

THE BRIDGE SCHOOL

San Francisco Bay Blues
Pretty Boy Floyd
With God on Our Side
Girl from the North Country
Gates of Eden
Forever Young

The Neil Young Bridge School Benefits were an annual event from 1986 until 2016 when he canceled the event, likely due to his divorce from wife Pegi, who co-produced the annual event. The concerts were all acoustic evenings of music to benefit the school. According to the website bridgeschool.org:

> The Bridge School is a non-profit organization whose mission is to ensure that individuals with severe speech and physical impairments achieve full participation in their communities through the use of augmentative & alternative means of communication (AAC) and assistive technology (AT) applications and through the development, implementation and dissemination of innovative life-long educational strategies. The Bridge School is an internationally recognized leader in the education of children who use augmentative and alternative communication and has developed unique programs and trained highly skilled professionals in the use of state of the art assistive technology.

The annual event, lasting through the weekend, featured major stars in an acoustic setting. Artists included: Paul McCartney, Brian Wilson, the Foo Fighters, James Taylor, the Wallflowers, R.E.M., Lou Reed, Metallica, Lucinda Williams, Simon & Garfunkel, Tom Petty and the Heartbreakers, and so many more.

160

The earliest concerts were held at the Oakland Coliseum but moved to the Shoreline Amphitheatre in Mountain View. This performance is just Bob and G. E. Smith on acoustic guitars. It's typical of the acoustic set Bob and G. E. did in the middle of their standard shows, and as with those great shows of the Never Ending Tour, all performances are great. Also, the sound is great, as it comes from a soundboard recording. Very highly recommended, especially as a companion to the 1988 leg of the Never Ending Tour.

CDs:
- **Blown Out on the Trail**

Grateful Dead Jam 1989
The Forum
Los Angeles, California
February 12, 1989

Iko-Iko
Monkey and the Engineer
Alabama Getaway
Dire Wolf
Cassidy
Stuck Inside of Mobile with the Memphis
Blues Again
Not Fade Away
Knockin' on Heaven's Door

Dylan makes a guest appearance at a Grateful Dead concert, but he mostly sits in on guitar, except for a brief vocal on "Memphis Blues Again" and the lead vocal on "Knockin' on Heaven's Door". The sound is excellent, as is the norm for all Grateful Dead concerts. The entire performance lasts about an hour. If you like the Dead, you'll want to hear this just for them, otherwise be aware that the Dylan content is minimal.

Never Ending Tour Rehearsals 1989
New York City, New York
The Power Station
May 1989

Bob Dylan - guitar
G. E. Smith - guitar
Kenny Aaronson - bass
Christopher Parker - drums
Mindy Jostyn - harmonica, violin, & vocal

I Shall Be Released
Making Believe
Early Morning Rain
Shot of Love
Give My Love to Rose
Man Gave Names to All the Animals
(I Heard That) Lonesome Whistle
Both Sides Now
Too Far Gone
California Blues
Little Queen of Spades
I'm Not Supposed to Care
Not Fade Away
Everyday
When Did You Leave Heaven?
Everybody's Movin'
I'll Remember You
Ballad of a Thin Man
Peace in the Valley
Shelter from the Storm
Most Likely You Go Your Way (and I'll Go Mine)
Just Like Tom Thumb's Blues
Tomorrow Is a Long Time
Silvio

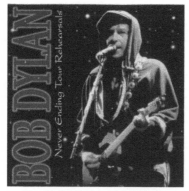

This excellent sounding studio rehearsal tape for the 1989 European portion of the Never Ending Tour began to circulate in 1996 when it appeared on the bootleg *The Never Ending Tour Rehearsals*. Very unusual with the addition of Mindy Jostyn on various instruments, including violin which gives the band a sort of "Desire" feel. Was he really thinking of adding a violin player to the mix? I think that would have been a great addition myself. The entire tape is about an hour and a half and is well worth seeking out.

CDs:
- **The Never Ending Tour Rehearsals**

Never Ending Tour 1989

The 1989 tour was pretty much exactly like the 1988 tour, except that there would be a change of lineup when Tony Garnier replaced Kenny Aaronson on bass, a position in which he remains to this day. In September *Oh Mercy* would be released, so the shows after that date featured songs from that album. Although there are a good number of excellent audience tapes from this leg of the tour, I am unaware of any soundboards in circulation. It should also be noted that by this time every single show was being recorded by someone somewhere. There is a good bet that if you were trying to collect every single show from the Never Ending Tour, you could probably do it. One thing that does distinguish the 1989 tour from 1988 is the relative looseness of the affair. Bob, in particular, was stretching a bit on guitar and often intros and endings would provide some unexpected surprises. They were starting to sound a little more like a jam band.

A word about *Oh Mercy* here. There are not many outtakes from the sessions in circulation, so I will not discuss it in a separate section. There *were* outtakes in circulation, but the release of the Bootleg Series entry *Tell Tale Signs* pretty much officially released those tracks and more. *Oh Mercy* was considered to be a major comeback for Dylan, and rightly so. Unlike the previous two albums, it consisted of all original material, and pretty good material at that. Produced by Daniel Lanois and recorded in New Orleans with, among others, members of the Neville Brothers. Why he chose not to record with his touring band is somewhat of a mystery, but the results certainly proved that he was right. The sound was swampy and mysterious – not something that his touring band was noted for. Obviously, *Oh Mercy* marked a turning point for Dylan.

Recommended shows:

Stockholm – May 28, 1989
Globe Arena
Stockholm, Sweden

Dylan seems to forget how to play some of these songs. The result is a fresh approach to some old favorites. Audience recording.

The Hague – June 10, 1989
Statenhal
The Hague, The Netherlands

First show with Tony Garnier, who is still with the band, making him the longest lasting member of Bob's touring band ever. The tape I have heard is a mediocre audience recording, but still it's worth hearing for Tony's debut.

CDs:
* **Live at Statenhal**

Frejus – June 13, 1989
Les Arènes
Frejus, France

Pretty good audience recording, if a little bit noisy on the crowd's part. One especially annoying crowd member kept calling for "Gates of Eden". He actually got his request. Because the concert is in France, Bob performs "Man Gave Names to All the Animals", since that song was something of a hit there. Ringo Starr guests on the last two songs before the encore.

Columbia – July 19, 1989
Marjorie Merriweather Post Pavilion
Columbia, Maryland

This is one of the best audience recordings I've ever heard. It also happens to be the first show from the Never Ending Tour that I ever heard. When I received it in a trade long ago, I was truly startled by what I heard. I think the last live material I had heard was the previous tour with Tom Petty. I had heard good things about the new lineup, but I wasn't expecting what I heard. One thing that stood out for me was the amount of guitar playing Bob was doing and how effective it was as an accompaniment to G. E. Smith's pretty amazing rocking leads.

Berkeley – September 3, 1989
Greek Theatre
University Of California
Berkeley, California

One of the best 1989 shows. Some unusual numbers, such as "Lonely Is a Man Without Love", for an instrumental opener, and Jimmy Cliff's "The Harder They Come". Audience recording.

Los Angeles – September 9, 1989
Greek Theatre
Hollywood
Los Angeles, California

Another outstanding show from the fall 1989 tour. Opens with a rare "Visions of Johanna". Another good audience recording.

Chabad Telethon 1989
Los Angeles, California
September 24, 1989

Einsleipt Mein Kind Dein Eigalach
Adelita
Hava Negeilah

Bob Dylan performs with Harry Dean Stanton and Peter Himmelman at the 25th anniversary L'Chaim – To Life!, Telethon '89. Because it was broadcast on TV, good mono copies exist. About 10 minutes total. Calling themselves "Chopped Liver", Bob only plays harmonica on "Hava Negeilah". Bob plays recorder and Stanton plays harmonica on Adelita. If you're a completist, you should seek this out, which at this writing is easily found on the Internet in rather poor quality. Otherwise, don't bother.

Never Ending Tour 1990

Again, more of the same from the previous two years, although we would see G. E. Smith leave the band after the run of shows at Radio City Music Hall in New York City in October. G. E.'s last show was October 19, 1990, after which he was replaced by two guitarists – John Staehely (Jo Jo Gunne, Spirit, The Staehely Brothers) and César Diaz (Dylan's guitar tech). In a lot of ways, the 1990 tour was the peak of the first Never Ending Tour shows. Although not as fist-in-your-face rocking as 1988, it's a little tighter than 1989. There was also an attempt to shake things up a bit with some more unusual song choices. *Oh Mercy* was being heavily promoted, and towards the end of the year more songs from *Under the Red Sky* were being performed.

Recommended shows:

New Haven – January 12, 1990
Toad's Place
New Haven, Connecticut

This show is notable for being the longest show of the Never Ending Tour, but actually it might be a mistake to consider it a part of the tour proper. For one thing, it wasn't a concert, per se. It was four sets in a club called Toad's Place in New Haven, and it seemed to serve as more of a live rehearsal or dry run for some new songs and a possible new approach to the tour. The other thing that marks this as different, apart from the length, was the absence of acoustic numbers. It's all electric and a lot of unusual songs were tried out for the first, and in some cases last time. Songs like "Walk a Mile in My Shoes", "Dancing in the Dark" (the Bruce Springsteen song), "Help Me Make It Through the Night", and others. The recording is very good and the audience is enthusiastic, which gives a lot of energy to Bob and the band. The performances are inspired and Bob in particular is in very good form.

Blown Out on the Trail

CDs:
- **Toad's Place Volumes 1 and 2**

Penn State – January 14, 1990
Pennsylvania State University
State College, Pennsylvania

Like the Toad's Place show on the 12th, this concert was completely electric without any acoustic numbers at all. The tape I have is a fairly decent audience recording, if a little trebly. Apparently this experiment wasn't to his liking because he changed the format for the next show. For the next night's show he opened with a full band number ("Watching the River Flow") and then went immediately to the short acoustic set before returning to the electric portion.

Rio de Janeiro – January 25, 1990
Sambodromo
Rio de Janeiro, Brazil

The only soundboard tape from the 1990 tour that I know of. Dylan rarely played South America, so this was most unusual. Some of the show was broadcast on television in Brazil. It's not the best soundboard I have heard, with the mix being poor and some instruments fading in and out. Still, it's the only soundboard from 1990 that I know of.

CDs:
- **Rio**

Montreal – May 29, 1990
University Of Montreal
Montreal, Quebec, Canada

This has long been one of my favorite shows from the 1990 tour. The high point for me is "No More One More Time", which was a debut. For that one performance alone, this tape is worth seeking out. The recording is good, but of course we have to contend with a noisy crowd.

170

La Crosse – June 12, 1990
Civic Center
La Crosse, Wisconsin

Another great show from Spring of 1990. Good audience recording.
The band is in great form on this.

West Point – October 13, 1990
Eisenhower Hall Theater
West Point, New York

One of the best shows from the 1990 tour. It's an excellent audience
tape, and for once the noisy crowd is actually appreciated for their
enthusiasm, especially on the opening number "Tangled Up in
Blue". The audience members closest to the microphone are
amusing to listen to as one person yells out "That's Robert! There's
Robert!" and later, during G. E.'s first solo, "GEEE EEEE!" Of
course, the best thing about this show is the rendition of "Masters
of War" being performed at the military academy. The band seems
to be in especially great form, perhaps knowing that very shortly
G. E.'s term would be coming to an end. By this time a second
guitarist, César Diaz, was added to the mix. He would remain,
along with John Staehely, for the remainder of 1990. A complete
video of the show is also in circulation.

Tom Petty Jam 1990
Los Angeles, California
The Forum
March 1, 1990

Rainy Day Women # 12 & 35
Everybody's Movin'
Travelin' Band
I'm Crying

Bob makes a guest appearance with Tom Petty and the Heartbreakers. It's a poor quality audience recording with a lot of crowd noise. On "Travelin' Band" and "I'm Crying" Bruce Springsteen sings while Bob just plays guitar. Not really recommended, unless you're a completist.

Traveling Wilburys Sessions 1990
Los Angeles, California
April 1990

Sessions for the 2nd Wilburys album took place in April. By this time, Roy Orbison had already passed away and so they decided not to replace him with another member, although I personally thought Johnny Cash would have been a good candidate. Rough mixes are in circulation with Bob singing much more than appeared on the eventual album. One reason for having so much Dylan vocal present was because he was constantly on the road and no one was sure what his availability might be for overdubs, so they just had him sing pretty much everything with the idea in mind that he could be mixed down or out if one of the other singers was to be featured ("will bury it in the mix?"). The rough mix tape, if you can find it, makes for a nice alternative to the official album.

Never Ending Tour 1991

As far as I'm concerned, the 1991 tour represented the absolute low point in the Never Ending Tour. John Staehely was out and John Jackson became the permanent replacement from 1991 throughout 1996. I know Jackson has many supporters, but I always found him to be a rather dull and unimaginative guitarist, but maybe that's what Bob was looking for after the flash of G. E. Smith. Jackson certainly had his moments, but overall I got the impression of a very technically competent player who could play all the notes but just didn't feel them. The other big difference in the lineup was the loss of Christopher Parker, one of the best drummers he's ever played with. He was replaced by Ian Wallace, who had played with Bob during the 1978 tour. Certainly Wallace is a fine drummer, but there's just something about the excitement that Christopher Parker brought that was missing.

Compared to the G. E. years, the 1991 shows were often very sloppy and unlistenable. Bob has to take the blame for this, in my opinion, because it appears that during this time his drinking had become a problem. He often appeared drunk on stage, and it was apparent in many of the tapes I have heard.

By this time they were promoting *Under the Red Sky*, as they had during the final shows of 1990. After the great positive reception given to *Oh Mercy*, and the career comeback it afforded, the highly anticipated *Under the Red Sky* was not very well received by critics and fans and was perceived to be a major disappointment. Personally, I think the album has been treated unfairly and I consider it to be an excellent album. Several things about the album came under harsh criticism. First, the production by Don Was. Fans trashed it. I think the production is excellent, and I thought so the very first time I heard the album on a pre-release cassette months before it was officially released. Another criticism was the material itself. Songs like "Wiggle Wiggle" and "2 x 2" were singled out as being childish nonsense unworthy of the great Bob Dylan. I was surprised to hear this when the album was released because it seemed obvious to me what he was doing: nursery rhymes for adults. I didn't see anything wrong with that, and thought it was quite innovative. Finally, another unwarranted criticism was the inclusion of famous guest artists as sidemen: George Harrison, Elton John, David Crosby, Slash. As if there was something inherently wrong with including these musicians, as if he were trying to gain some sort of commercial acceptance by recording a song with Elton John or George Harrison, but honestly would anyone have known that Elton John was playing piano or George Harrison playing guitar if they hadn't been told so? Of much more importance to me was the group of musicians assembled by Don Was to provide backup: Stevie Ray Vaughan, Jimmy Vaughan, Al Kooper, Randy Jackson, Kenny Aronoff, Don Was himself. One of the best backup bands ever put together for a Bob Dylan album, and yet all anyone could do was complain about "Wiggle Wiggle". Obviously, I've always loved this album, but that's no doubt a minority opinion.

All that being said, he didn't really perform very many songs from the album during the 1991 shows. "Wiggle Wiggle", "God Knows", and "Under the Red Sky" were played more often than any others from the album.

Since 1991 is my least favorite of the Never Ending Tour years, I can't really recommend many shows. I will attempt to single out a few that would be good to hear for an idea of what a shambles it was. Some of them rise above shambles, though.

Zürich – January 28, 1991
Hallenstadion
Zürich, Switzerland

The first show with John Jackson, and it doesn't start well. The announcer introduces them as "Bob Dylan and his sons". Then they

175

launch into a shambolic unrehearsed version of "Most Likely You Go Your Way (and I'll Go Mine)". It's a rather muddy sounding audience tape, but you really should hear it for an example of what was to come. It seemed that after the great Dylan renaissance of 1988-1990, it had all come to an end.

Williamsport – February 21, 1991
Capitol Theater
Williamsport, Pennsylvania

I think this is the best of the early '91 shows and the one to have if you only need one show to represent this period. Strong performances overall. Still, subpar compared to the previous years of the Never Ending Tour. Decent audience recording, which helps a bit, but the crowd is noisy and there seems to be a lot of laughter and conversation, which is annoying.

Ringe – June 19, 1991
Midtfyns Festival
Ringe, Denmark

Partial soundboard tape (first song missing) but still a pretty awful sounding performance. Not much to recommend other than the fact it's a soundboard recording and worth hearing just for that. If you really need a 1991 show for your collection, this will do. The band really tries to do the best with what they have and John Jackson does shine in some moments, but mostly it could have been anyone playing the solos.

Wolf Trap – July 20, 1991
Wolf Trap Farm Park For The Performing Arts
Filene Center
Vienna, Virginia

Another soundboard, this time from Wolf Trap and taken from a sound system for the hearing-impaired. As such, the mix is pretty good and the entire show is listenable. Maybe by this time the band was getting more comfortable playing this material, and Bob tended to sit things out a bit more, giving the band more room to stretch.

Tulsa – October 30, 1991
Brady Theater
Tulsa, Oklahoma

The last of the 1991 soundboards, this one available on the CD *Answer Me*. Steve Ripley guests on some songs.

Evanston – November 11, 1991
McCaw Hall
The Northwestern University
Evanston, Illinois

This is more like it! Excellent show in excellent sound for an audience tape. Remember, though, that you should lower your expectations when listening to any 1991 show.

Grammy Awards 1991
New York City, New York
Radio City Music Hall
February 20, 1991

Masters of War

Bob Dylan with his touring band played "Masters of War" and then accepted a lifetime achievement award at the 1991 Grammy Awards ceremony. First Jack Nicholson gives an amusing introduction – "this guy's a riot in more ways than one". Since it

was broadcast on CBS-TV, excellent video and audio exists. Many people have criticized his performance as indecipherable, but I find it to be pretty good. His speech after the performance is famous for its bizarre content, but one thing that should be pointed out is that this performance came right at the beginning of the first Gulf War and the choice of "Masters of War" must have certainly been deliberate and pointed.

His speech consisted of the following: "Thank You ... well ... alright ... yeah, well, my daddy he didn't leave me too much ... you know he was a very simple man and he didn't leave me a lot but what he told me was this ... what he did say was ... son ... he said uh .... he said so many things ya know ..... he said you know it's possible to become so defiled in this world that your own mother and father will abandon you, and if that happens God will always believe in your own ability to mend your ways."

Since it was a TV broadcast, excellent audio and video copies are in wide circulation.

Chabad Telethon 1991
Los Angeles, California
September 15, 1991

Sold American

Bob backs up Kinky Friedman on electric guitar and also gives a short pitch to the audience to donate to what he says is his favorite charity. If you like Kinky Friedman, you will like this performance. Bob's electric accompaniment is not bad at all. There's not much to say other than that. Audio and video are easily found on the Internet (as of this writing).

Guitar Legends Festival 1991
Seville, Spain
Auditorio de la Cartuja
October 17 1991

Bob Dylan - guitar & vocal
Phil Manzanera - guitar
Richard Thompson - guitar
Jack Bruce - bass
Ray Cooper - percussion
Simon Phillips - drums
Keith Richards - guitar
Steve Cropper - guitar
Edward Manion - saxophone
Chuck Leavell - keyboards
Charlie Drayton - bass
Steve Jordan - drums

All Along the Watchtower
Boots of Spanish Leather
Across the Borderline
Answer Me, My Love
Shake, Rattle and Roll
I Can't Turn You Loose

According to Wikipedia:

> Guitar Legends was a concert held over five nights, from October 15 to October 19, 1991, in Seville, Spain, with the aim of positioning the city as an entertainment destination to draw support for Expo '92 beginning the following April.

Participants, in addition to Bob, were Keith Richards, Phil Manzanera, Joe Walsh, Richard Thompson, Les Paul, Steve Cropper, Robbie Robertson, Larry Coryell, BB King, and many other fine guitarists.

Both Richard Thompson and Phil Manzanera provide excellent guitar solos on "All Along the Watchtower" while Bob is backed up with an all-star band that also includes Jack Bruce and Keith Richards. It's a rare treat to hear Bob backed up by the always excellent Richard Thompson. This is from an article in Uncut magazine by Michael Bonner. Phil Manzanera, who was the musical director for this event, says:

> I knew he liked Richard Thompson, so I rang up Richard who was playing in Holland or somewhere, and said "Richard, would you like to play with Dylan?" "Yeah sure!" He arrived, so I sent him in before the concert to find out what numbers Bob was going to do. He came out and said, "Right, we're doing this and this…" So we went on stage. The manager had said, "If Bob does come on, make sure you introduce him." So we went on stage – "It's Bob Dylan!" – and of course he doesn't play any of the numbers we rehearsed. We're all looking at each other, wondering what key he was playing… But you know, he's a genius. So who cares…

Richard Thompson has a slightly different story, and reportedly his disappointment with the way things went led him to write "Put It

There Pal". From the liner notes to the 5-CD set *A History of Richard Thompson*:

> Bob Dylan was one of Richard's greatest passions from his earliest days in Fairport Convention (when a photo of Bob Dylan graced the walls of their rehearsal studio). So when Dylan's manager put in a call for Richard to accompany Bob Dylan during a live show in Seville, Spain, in the mid-nineties entitled something like "Classics of the Guitar," Richard immediately said yes. He flew out on short notice and found on his arrival that Dylan refused to see him or rehearse before the show, and so they met onstage. Richard had no idea what songs Dylan was going to perform, or even what key the songs would be in, and so spent most of his time retuning his guitar onstage and feeling like a fool. But, hey, we get one of Richard's most passionately bitter vocals and angry and blistering guitar solos.

Richard Thompson accompanies Bob on three acoustic numbers. I think overall, Thompson was being a little harsh on himself. He sounds great throughout and nothing really sounds unrehearsed.

Since this was broadcast live a very nice stereo FM tape exists of this set of performances as well as a complete video.

David Letterman 10ᵗʰ Anniversary Show
New York City, New York
Radio City Music Hall
January 18, 1992

Bob Dylan - vocal & guitar
Chrissie Hynde - guitar, harmony vocals
Carole King - piano
Steve Vai - guitar
Sid Mcginnsss – guitar
Edgar Winter - saxophone
Doc Severinsen - trumpet
Jim Horn - baritone saxophone
Maceo Parker - alto saxophone
Fred Wesley & Pee Wee Ellis - trombone
Jim Keltner - drums
Paul Schaffer - Hammond organ
Will Lee - bass
Anton Fig - drums
Rosanne Cash, Nancy Griffith, Emmylou Harris, Michelle Shocked, Mavis
Staples - backup vocals

Like a Rolling Stone

In January of 1992, David Letterman was celebrating the 10ᵗʰ anniversary of his late night talk show on NBC-TV. This was the show that aired after the Tonight Show, which had long been the top rated late night talk show hosted by Johnny Carson.

When Carson retired in 1992, Letterman was passed over as the new host – a job he rightfully felt he was entitled to after serving ten years in waiting – and went to CBS for a late night show that directly competed with the new Tonight Show. He stayed there

183

until his own retirement in 2015. But for this show, he pulled out all the stops and presented as his special musical guest, Bob Dylan and a crazy array of superstars supplanting the David Letterman house band led by Paul Schaffer. Musically, it sounds great, if a little bland, but Bob himself sounded less than inspired. It added yet more fuel to the "Bob Dylan is a washed-up has-been" meme that had been going around since the early '80s.

The sound is great, being that it was broadcast well into the era of digital home recording, so it shouldn't be too hard to find.

Never Ending Tour 1992

1992 found the band changing again, this time with the addition of Bucky Baxter on pedal steel guitar and Winston Watson added on drums, along with Ian Wallace (two drummers!). Later, Charile Quintana would replace Ian Wallace as the second drummer for the remainder of the 1992 shows. Bucky Baxter, formerly with Steve Earle, was a major asset to the live ensemble and the 1992 shows were an improvement over the previous year. It could be also that Bob had managed to get his drinking under control, because overall he seemed more focused and committed to the material. There was really no new album to promote at this time, seeing as *Good As I Been to You* would not be released until the end of the year, so there were a lot more songs from *Under the Red Sky* as well the usual set list with a few surprises thrown in.

Recommended shows:

Melbourne – April 3, 1992
Palais Theatre
Melbourne, Victoria, Australia

Pretty good audience recording of a typical early 1992 show, this one noted for the first "Idiot Wind" since the Rolling Thunder Revue in 1976. The other Melbourne shows were pretty good too, as was the rest of the Australian tour. A big improvement over the previous year.

Waikiki – April 24, 1992
Waikiki Shell
Waikiki, Hawaii

The only soundboard from the 1992 tour in circulation. Average performance with very good sound. This was the last show with Ian Wallace on drums. Starting in Seattle, Charlie Quintana would replace Wallace as the second drummer.

CDs:
- **Paradise, Hawaiian Style**

The early part of the US tour proved a little disappointing. I won't go into any great detail on them, but I can only recommend the following:

Seattle, Washington – April 28, 1992
San Francisco, California – May 5, 1992
San Jose, California – May 9, 1992

The late '92 shows were truly incredible, mostly thanks to the new drummer Winston Watson. The best:

Binghampton, New York – October 12, 1992
Providence, Rhode Island – October 25, 1992
Wilkes-Barre, Pennsylvania – November 1, 1992
Youngstown, Ohio – November 2, 1992
Sarasota, Florida – November 9, 1992
Clearwater, Florida – November 11, 1992

David Bromberg Sessions
Acme Recording, Chicago - June 1992

Bob Dylan - vocal & guitar
David Bromberg - guitar
Peter Ecklund - trumpet
John Firmin - tenor saxophone & clarinet
Curtis Lindberg - trombone
Glen Lowe - guitar
Dick Fegy - fiddle & mandolin
Jeff Wisor - fiddle & mandolin
Christopher Cameron - keyboards
Robert Amiot - bass
Richard Crooks - drums
Chicago South Side Gospel Choir - vocals

I'll Rise Again
Nobody's Fault but Mine
The Lady Came From Baltimore
Polly Vaughan
Casey Jones
Duncan and Brady
Catskills Serenade
World of Fools
Miss the Mississippi and You
Sloppy Drunk
Hey Joe
Northeast Texas Woman

One of the great lost albums of all time. Why it wasn't released still remains a mystery to me. In its place Dylan released *Good As I Been to You* instead. "Duncan and Brady" and "Miss the Mississippi and You" were both officially released on *Tell Tale Signs*, but the rest remain unreleased. Aside from the released tracks, the others that are in general circulation consist of "Polly Vaughn", "Catskills Serenade", and "Sloppy Drunk". I'm hoping for an official release someday, but that day may be long off. The sound is excellent, as you would expect from a studio recording session.

Clinton Inaugural and Blue Jeans Bash
Washington DC, January 17 1993

In 1992, the Presidential election between incumbent George Bush and challenger Bill Clinton was decided in Clinton's favor. The new President was not sworn in until January, and so the usual inauguration ceremonies took place in Washington DC. As is normal, entertainment is provided, along with speeches and the swearing-in ceremony. Dylan's involvement is as follows.

Washington DC
Lincoln Memorial
January 17, 1993
President Bill Clinton inauguration

Chimes of Freedom

Bob Dylan made a surprise appearance at the inauguration ceremonies at the Lincoln Memorial performing "Chimes of Freedom" with a band led by Quincy Jones. It was broadcast on TV, so it shouldn't be too hard to find good quality audio and video.

Washington DC
National Building Museum
January 17, 1993
The Absolutely Unofficial Blue Jeans Bash

Bob Dylan - guitar
Stephen Stills - guitar
Rick Danko - bass
Garth Hudson - keyboards
Levon Helm - drums
Jimmy Weider - guitar
Richard Bell - piano
Randy Ciarlante - drums
Ronnie Hawkins - guitar
Don Johnson - guitar
The Cate Brothers

To Be Alone with You
Key to the Highway
I Shall Be Released
(I Don't Want To) Hang Up My Rock and Roll Shoes

This event took place on the same day as the Clinton inauguration. It was open to the public, but only if you were a resident of Arkansas! Clinton was, of course, Governor of Arkansas before becoming President and many of the musicians at this event were from Arkansas – Levon Helm, Ronnie Hawkins, and the Cate Brothers. It's basically a jam session.

This is an excellent sounding stereo soundboard lasting twenty minutes, but only the first song features Bob on vocal, so the rest is

189

only of interest to hear the rest of this jam. The performance of "To Be Alone with You" sounds really good, as it should considering the musicians involved. I have not heard the rest, so I can't comment on the merits of the other songs, but I imagine it's worth hearing. By the way, Dylan doesn't sing "I Shall Be Released" as expected. It's the Cate Brothers.

Never Ending Tour 1993

The 1993 shows were more or less the same as 1992, except that Winston Watson was the only drummer now. Since *World Gone Wrong* had just been released in October, it was somewhat being promoted, especially at the Supper Club shows (see next entry for more details). Although better than 1992 and certainly better than 1991, the shows still left plenty to be desired, but things were getting a little better for Dylan and his live performances.

Sometime in the 2000's a huge cache of what has been termed "pre-boards" of the 1993 tour came into circulation. The story goes that they were all taped by a member of Bob's road crew and only came into circulation after his death. Though given the meaningless term "pre-boards", they are most likely monitor mixes, which would explain the wide disparity in mix quality from tape to tape. Some are very good mixes where others emphasize vocals over instruments and others vice versa. There are 40 known "pre-boards":

> **Dublin, Ireland – February 5**
> **London, England – February 7**
> **London, England – February 9**
> **London, England – February 11**
> **London, England – February 12**
> **London, England – February 13**
> **Utrecht, The Netherlands – February 15**
> **Utrecht, The Netherlands – February 16**
> **Eindhoven, The Netherlands – February 17**
> **Hannover, Germany – February 18**
> **Wiesbaden, Germany – February 20**
> **Petange, Luxembourg – February 21**
> **Paris, France – February 23**
> **Belfast, Northern Ireland – February 25**
> **Nashville, Tennessee – April 13**
> **Nashville, Tennessee – April 14**

Radford, Virginia – April 16
Knoxville, Tennessee – April 17
Asheville, North Carolina – April 18
Huntsville, Alabama – April 19
Monroe, Louisiana – April 21
New Orleans, Louisiana – April 23
London, England – June 12
Tel-Aviv, Israel – June 17
Beersheba, Israel – June 19
Haifa, Israel – June 20
Athens, Greece – June 22
Athens, Greece – June 23
Pisa, Italy – June 26
Marseille, France – June 29
Toulouse, France – June 30
Barcelona, Spain – July 1
Vitoria, Spain – July 2
Waterford, Ireland – July 4
Huesca, Spain – July 6
Gijon, Spain – July 8
La Coruna, Spain – July 9
Mérida, Spain – July 12
Cascais, Portugal – July 13, 19
Bern, Switzerland – July 17

There were also plenty of decent sounding audience tapes.

Of special note was Bob co-headlining with Santana, which took place August through October.

Recommended shows:

Marseilles – June 29, 1993
Palais des Sports
Marseilles, France

One of the "pre-boards", this one released on the bootleg CD *Hard Times in Marseilles*. It's an obvious monitor mix because you have a hard time hearing some of the instruments. Still, it's a beautifully

192

clear recording that lets you hear the nuances of the band, which was improving quite a bit over the previous two years.

Barcelona – July 1, 1993
El Pueblo Español
Barcelona, Spain

One of the line recordings listed above. This one is a particularly good one and the show itself is a pretty good representation of a typical 1993 show, but perhaps a little better than expected.

Wolf Trap – September 8-9, 1993
Filene Center
Wolf Trap Farm Park
Vienna, Virginia

The September 8 show is available both as an audience recording and a rough soundboard. Notable for the first appearance of "Series of Dreams". The audience tape sounds much better, but it's good to have both. The September 9 soundboard fades in and out, but there is a complete audience recording in circulation. As was the case for the previous night, the audience recording may be more satisfying to listen to.

Supper Club Shows 1993
New York City
The Supper Club
November 16-17 1993

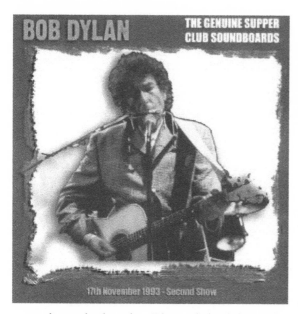

17th November 1993 - Second Show

The series of shows at the Supper Club in New York City has taken on a legendary status that merits a special entry apart from the Never Ending Tour sections. Unlike the typical concerts given in 1993 with the same group of musicians, the format was entirely acoustic instead of a combination of acoustic and electric. The original intention of these shows was, purportedly, to film an episode of *MTV Unplugged* featuring Bob Dylan. However, none of these shows made it to the final broadcast, if indeed they were ever actually intended for that show. Ultimately, what happened was that Bob and company went into the studio a year later to film an acoustic performance for *MTV Unplugged* in what was considered by many fans to be far inferior to the Supper Club shows. Certainly, the Supper Club shows featured a more non-typical set list as opposed to the usual concert, and the real intention appears to be a promotion for the then current album *World Gone Wrong*.

I'm not sure I entirely agree with the common wisdom that these shows were better than *MTV Unplugged*, but they certainly are great just the same and helped to raise Bob's profile and demonstrated that he was perhaps heading for yet another career high.

There were four shows altogether, over two days, with an afternoon show followed by an evening show. The set lists were similar but were also full of surprises. Who would have expected acoustic versions of "Tight Connection to My Heart" or "Queen Jane Approximately"? Among the *World Gone Wrong* songs included are "Blood in My Eyes", "Ragged and Dirty", and "Jack-A-Roe". Originally, only audience recordings circulated, but at some point the complete soundboards became available. Your best bet is to find *The Genuine Supper Club Shows*.

Recommended: All of them. Do I have a favorite? Not really, but if forced to choose I would probably go with the final evening show of the 17th.

November 16 Early Show

Absolutely Sweet Marie
Lay Lady Lay
Blood in My Eyes
Queen Jane Approximately
Tight Connection to My Heart
Disease of Conceit
I Want You
Ring Them Bells
My Back Pages
Forever Young

November 16 Late Show

Ragged and Dirty
Lay Lady Lay
I'll Be Your Baby Tonight
Queen Jane Approximately

Jack-A-Roe
One Too Many Mornings
I Want You
Ring Them Bells
My Back Pages
Forever Young

November 17 Early Show

Ragged and Dirty
One More Cup of Coffee
Blood in My Eyes
Queen Jane Approximately
I'll Be Your Baby Tonight
Disease of Conceit
I Want You
Ring Them Bells
My Back Pages
Forever Young

November 17 Late Show

Ragged and Dirty
Lay Lady Lay
Tight Connection to My Heart
Weeping Willow
Delia
Jim Jones
Queen Jane Approximately
Ring Them Bells
Jack-A-Roe
Forever Young
I Shall Be Released

CDs:
* **The Genuine Supper Club Shows**

David Letterman Show 1993
New York City – November 18, 1993

Forever Young

After the successful Supper Club shows from the previous two days, Bob Dylan and band appeared on the David Letterman show to perform an acoustic version of "Forever Young" with Paul Schaeffer providing organ accompaniment. By this time, David Letterman had quit his previous late night show on NBC for the more prestigious 11:30 PM timeslot in direct competition with the Tonight Show, which by all rights should have been his. For a brief time, Letterman's show out rated his competition, but that wouldn't last. He lasted longer than anyone else in that time slot, against the Tonight Show, so that's saying something.

197

The performance is great. It sounds every bit as good as anything played at the Supper Club shows. Again, as we are now well into the modern digital era, high quality audio and video are available. I'm unaware of any official release as yet that contains this performance.

Never Ending Tour 1994

The band members remained consistent throughout the year, with the same lineup as the previous year. 1994 was a vast improvement and Bob gave some of the best shows of the '90s. There was no new album to promote, so the set lists were very similar to what had been before, but there were some new additions, such as "Jokerman" as a standard opener. All in all, it was a very good year for Dylan concerts and it was becoming clear that he was on an upward track to yet another major career revival.

It's hard to come up with a list of recommended shows, because so many of them are consistently great, but here are a few of my favorites:

Nagoya – February 2, 1994
Century Hall
Nagoya, Japan

A great recording of a great show. From the very first number ("Jokerman") Bob is on fire and fully engaged. No more 1991 type of performances. John Jackson was sounding better than ever. The whole band was cooking and the crowd was going wild. Also, a pretty damn good audience recording.

Hiroshima – February 16, 1994
Hiroshima Koseinenkin Kaikan
Hiroshima, Japan

Another great performance, although the tape doesn't sound as good as the Nagoya show from February 2.

Woodstock – August 14, 1994
Saugerties, New York

It was the 25th anniversary of Woodstock – an event that, although he lived there at the time, he did not participate in. There were rumors that he might make an appearance, especially since The Band was playing there, but for a number of reasons he did not. He did, however, appear at the Isle of Wight festival in 1969 with The Band, so he did not have an objection, per se, to appearing at a huge festival with his chosen group of musicians, so his snubbing of the Woodstock festival must have been a choice. Aside from this, the set list wasn't all that different from what he was normally doing in 1994 during the tour. The really nice thing about this is that it was broadcast on radio and television, so there are excellent quality boots of this performance equivalent to an official live album. Very highly recommended as a perfect example of what his live shows were like in 1994.

Lewiston – August 16, 1994
Art Park
Lewiston, New York

Nice soundboard, although it fades in during the opening number and takes a while to settle down into something truly listenable.

Roseland – October 20, 1994
Roseland Ballroom
New York City, New York

Bob played three shows at the Roseland Ballroom in New York City in October. All of them are pretty good, but I give the slight edge to this one.

Rhythm, Country & Blues Concert
Los Angeles – March 23, 1994

Bob Dylan - vocal & guitar
Trisha Yearwood - vocal & guitar
Randy Jacobs - guitar
Bernie Leadon - guitar
Charlie Musslewhite - harmonica
Mickie Raphael - keyboards
Benmont Tench – keyboards
Don Was - bass
Kenny Aronoff - drums
Robby Turner - backing vocal
Reggie Young - backing vocal
Lenny Castro - backing vocal
Sweet Pea Atkinson - backing vocal
Sir Harry Bowen - backing vocal

Tomorrow Night

Throughout the '80s and '90s Bob made a number of guest appearances in concert and on television. I think this is one of better ones. The purpose of this concert was largely to promote the MCA album "Rhythm, Country & Blues". It was  also a benefit for the Rhythm & Blues Foundation and the Country Music Foundation. For the concert, they gathered several duet combos from the album while adding, among others, Bob Dylan in a duet with Trisha Yearwood. Portions were broadcast on ABC-TV, which is why we have excellent audio and video of Bob's performance. We are certainly well into the digital age here, where

201

just about any performance is captured in some manner, and usually in excellent quality.

CDs:
- **Ring Them Bells: Unreleased Studio & Live Recordings, 1994**

The Great Music Experience
Nara, Japan
May 20-22, 1994

A Hard Rain's A-Gonna Fall
I Shall Be Released
Ring Them Bells
I Shall Be Released

This is one of the better one-off appearances by Dylan during his dry period, and it's one that greatly contributed to the redemption of his reputation during the '90s.

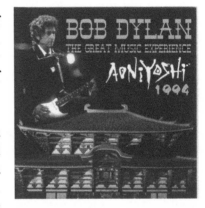

The Great Music Experience was a concert starring Japanese and international musicians staged at a Buddhist temple in Nara, Japan. The concert was held over three nights in May and was partly backed by UNESCO.

There were three shows, the first of which is available only as an audience recording, but the second two are available in excellent stereo PA quality due to the shows being broadcast on radio and television.

The performances are really amazing, with a full orchestra backing Bob singing his heart out on four songs. For the last song, he is joined by all of the other artists who participated in the event, including Joni Mitchell, Bon Jovi, Ry Cooder and the rest.

MTV Unplugged
New York City – November 15-18, 1994

MTV Unplugged is a show featuring acoustic performances by musical artists who are not normally associated with acoustic music. Usually, but not always rock & roll, artists who have appeared on the show include Paul McCartney, Eric Clapton, R.E.M., Neil Young, Nirvana, Tony Bennett, and so on. Early episodes did not necessarily focus on one particular artist and was more in the vein of a variety show, with the special consideration that the usually electric artists set aside their rock & roll instruments in favor of acoustic instruments, thus "Unplugged". One such show that comes to mind is the Smithereens with special guest Graham Parker.

As previously noted in the chapter about the Supper Club shows, many fans consider those to be far superior to the *MTV Unplugged* show being discussed here. I have a different opinion and don't see it that way at all. As good as those shows were, I don't think they would have made a very satisfying show for casual or non-fans. Instead of an emphasis on numbers from the *Good As I Been to You* and *World Gone Wrong* albums – albums that were clearly intended to present acoustic performances – the songs performed at the shows that were combined into the final broadcast were more along the line of songs from Bob's catalog that he did in most current shows, mixed in with some unusual numbers rarely performed. Sure, he did songs that most people associate with his acoustic-folk years ("The Times They Are A-Changin'" and "With God on Our Side", for instance), they were not necessarily songs that were always done in that fashion. The result was a fine mixture of old with new with some dramatically different arrangements in some cases.

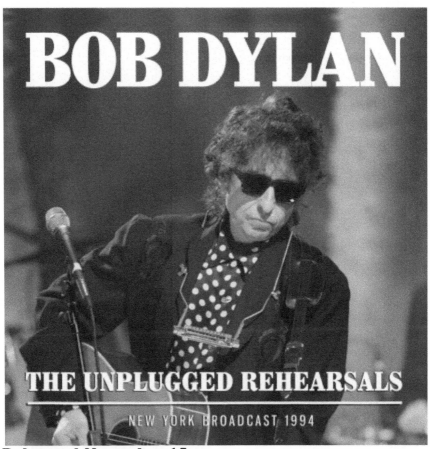

Rehearsal November 15

I Want You
Tombstone Blues
Don't Think Twice, It's All Right
Desolation Row
Hazel
Everything Is Broken
The Times They Are A-Changin'
Love Minus Zero/No Limit
Dignity
With God on Our Side

205

Rehearsal November 16

Absolutely Sweet Marie
Don't Think Twice, It's All Right
Desolation Row
Tombstone Blues
Hazel
Everything Is Broken
The Times They Are A-Changin'
Love Minus Zero/No Limit
Dignity
With God on Our Side
Desolation Row
Knockin' on Heaven's Door
I Pity the Poor Immigrant
Shooting Star

First Taping Session November 17:

Tombstone Blues
I Want You
Don't Think Twice, It's All Right
Desolation Row
Hazel
Everything Is Broken

The Times They Are A-Changin'
Love Minus Zero/No Limit
Dignity
With God on Our Side

Second Taping Session November 17:

Absolutely Sweet Marie
Shooting Star
All Along the Watchtower
My Back Pages
Rainy Day Women #12 & 35
John Brown
The Times They Are A-Changin'
Dignity
Knockin' on Heaven's Door
Like a Rolling Stone
Tonight I'll Be Staying Here with You
Desolation Row
I Want You

When the album was released in May of 1995, Dylan had his best selling album in years. It reached #23 in the US and #10 in the UK. It gave him a surge in popularity, brought him new respect among non-fans, and gave him more exposure on the rock concert circuit. The UK release had a bonus track that the US version didn't have: "Love Minus Zero/No Limit".

Never Ending Tour 1995

Not as good as the 1994 shows. For some reason, odd numbered years seem weaker than the even numbers. The band, although tighter than ever, are starting to get a little tired sounding. Winston Watson is especially irritating, lacking in dynamics, and John Jackson just seems to get worse. Still, some interesting shows and a new approach – Dylan dispenses with guitar for the beginning of many shows at the start of the European leg of the tour. It was suspected at the time that he might have been suffering from Carpal Tunnel Syndrome, due to the repetitious lead guitar patterns he was affecting. Of special note are two shows where Dylan opened for the Grateful Dead. Not only where they strong shows for Dylan, and in excellent sound quality, but they were some of Jerry Garcia's final shows and the last time Jerry and Bob played together live.

My recommendations:

Prague – March 11, 1995
Kongresový sál
Palác kultury
Prague, Czech Republic

First show to feature Dylan's new guitar-free style. Audience recording.

London – March 30, 1995
Brixton Academy
London, England

A favorite of many. This show best represents the early '95 shows. Elvis Costello guests on "I Shall Be Released".

Dublin – April 11, 1995
The Point Theatre
Dublin, Ireland

Of special interest for the presence of Carole King on piano throughout most of the show. Also making guest appearances were Van Morrison and Elvis Costello.

Laguna Seca – May 27, 1995
Laguna Seca Daze
Monterey, California

Excellent PA recording of a typical 1995 show. Nothing really wrong with that. It also appears to be professionally mixed and could very well have been an official release. Laguna Seca, by the way, is a racetrack in Monterey County in Northern California. It's an unusual venue for a concert. I've been there to see the occasional race. Available on the erroneously named bootleg CD *Laguna Beach*. Laguna Beach is an entirely different place in Southern California.

Washington DC – June 24 & 25 1995
RFK Stadium
Washington, D. C.

Fantastic soundboard recordings from the two shows Dylan opened for the Dead. By all accounts, Bob blew away the Dead. The 6/25 show has an appearance by Jerry Garcia during the encores. He died not long after.

Fort Lauderdale – September 23, 1995
The Edge
Fort Lauderdale, Florida

Open rehearsal in a small club in Fort Lauderdale. This show featured an almost entirely different set list than before or since. The choice of songs could almost be seen as a tribute to Jerry Garcia. The show is fresh and full of energy, something that was lacking in most other shows the same year. This is an absolute must. A pretty decent audience tape as well.

Rock & Roll Hall of Fame Museum Concert 1995
Cleveland, Ohio 1995
Cleveland Stadium
September 2, 1995

All Along the Watchtower
Just Like a Woman
Seeing the Real You at Last
Highway 61 Revisited
Forever Young

Bob Dylan and his touring band performed a brief set for the opening of the Rock & Roll Hall of Fame Museum. Bruce Springsteen guests on "Forever Young". "All Along the Watchtower" was officially released on *The Concert for the Rock*

and Roll Hall of Fame. Since the concert was broadcast live on television, excellent quality recordings exist.

CDs:
- **Big Bob & Holding Co.**
- **Seeing the Real You at Last**
- **Boys I'm Gonna Speak to the Crowd**
- **Forever Young**
- **I Am the Real Bob Dylan**
- **Loud and Strong**
- **Pledging My Time**
- **Laguna Beach**

Frank Sinatra 80th Birthday Tribute
Los Angeles, California
Shrine Auditorium
November 19, 1995

Restless Farewell

This 80th birthday tribute to Frank Sinatra was broadcast on television, so there are excellent quality PA tapes available as well as excellent video. Rather than perform a song made famous by Sinatra (rumors have it that he originally intended to sing "High Hopes"), he sang a song that certainly had great resonance for Sinatra given the lyrics ("and I'll bid farewell and not give a damn"), which perhaps reflected his attitude better than any other song that could have been sung. The performance is excellent and was widely praised.

Never Ending Tour 1996

The 1996 tour was not much better than the 1995 tour. The band was getting old and a change was needed. That would happen by the end of the year with the departure of Winston Watson and the arrival of David Kemper, formerly with the Jerry Garcia Band. It was no doubt the Jerry Garcia connection that brought him to Bob's attention.

Most of the shows pretty much sounded the same, so it's hard to recommend specific ones, but I will attempt to point some out that are either slightly unusual or worth hearing to get a sample of what the tour was like.

Recommended shows:

Liverpool – June 26 and 27, 1996
Empire
Liverpool, England

These shows are notable for the inclusion of Al Kooper on keyboards. Essentially a warmup for the Prince's Trust concert a few days later. Outstanding "Memphis Blues Again" with Kooper recreating his organ part on the original record.

Konstanz – July 3, 1996
Grosses Zelt
Klein Venedig
Konstanz, Germany

Dave Matthews and members of his band appear on a few songs. They opened for Dylan at this show. If you are a Dave Matthews fan, you'll probably want to hear this show.

Atlanta – August 3 and 4, 1996
House of Blues
Atlanta, Georgia

213

Two shows were professionally filmed at the House of Blues in Atlanta in August; therefore excellent sounding mono and stereo recordings are in circulation.

San Luis Obispo – October 17, 1996
Performing Arts Center
California Polytechnic State University
San Luis Obispo, California

First show with new drummer David Kemper, so it's of interest primarily because of that.

Mesa – October 20, 1996
Mesa Amphitheater
Mesa, Arizona

Nils Lofgren guests on a few numbers.

Austin – October 26 and 27, 1996
Austin Music Hall
Austin, Texas

Notable for the appearance of Charlie Sexton who sits in on a few numbers. Charlie Sexton would become a permanent member of the band sometime later and continues to play with Bob to this day (as of this writing).

The Prince's Trust – June 29, 1996
Hyde Park
London, England

Leopard-Skin Pill-Box Hat
All Along the Watchtower
Positively 4th Street
Just Like Tom Thumb's Blues
Tangled Up in Blue
Don't Think Twice, It's All Right
Silvio
Seven Days
Highway 61 Revisited

From Wikipedia: "The Prince's Trust is a charity in the United Kingdom founded in 1976 by Charles, Prince of Wales to help vulnerable young people get their lives on track. It supports 11 to 30-year-olds who are unemployed and those struggling at school and at risk of exclusion. Many of the young people helped by The Trust are in or leaving care, facing issues such as homelessness or mental health problems, or have been in trouble with the law."

As part of this charity, a concert was organized in Hyde Park. This concert featured appearances by The Who, Eric Clapton, and Alanis Morissette, among others. Both Ron Wood and Al Kooper join Dylan's band for this appearance, which is a shorter version of a

regular Dylan concert. Some of the concert was broadcast on HBO, which accounts for the excellent stereo sound quality of what was broadcast. There is also a mediocre audience tape of the entire

Dylan set. It was a good performance, especially nice because of the addition of Kooper and Wood. Kooper's keyboards add quite a lot to the sound and it's unfortunate that he didn't play more shows with them. Once you read Kooper's account of his brief stint with the band in his book *Backstage Passes & Bloodsucking Bastards*, you begin to understand why it didn't last, and he puts the blame squarely on Tony Garnier's shoulders. As musical director for Bob's band, Garnier told Kooper to lay off playing his signature riff on "Like a Rolling Stone". That, Kooper, says, is the equivalent of telling Keith Richards not to play his signature riff on "I Can't Get No Satisfaction". He considered Garnier to be insulting and unprofessional and it seems they didn't get along. It's too bad, because every time Kooper collaborated with Bob Dylan, something great always came of it.

Afterword

The two decades covered in this book saw a great variety of highs and lows; highs such as the albums *Desire* and *Slow Train Coming* and lows such as *Knocked out Loaded* and *Down in the Groove*. In the middle we saw such works as *Shot of Love* and *Infidels*. We saw two solo acoustic albums and *MTV Unplugged*. He was all over the place and full of surprises as well as disappointments. As for live performances, we had seen some wild variations in quality, but he was never lacking for great musicians. We saw him put together a slick big band for the 1978 world tour. We saw the various gospel bands that played with fire and brimstone, and we also saw collaborations with the Grateful Dead and Tom Petty and the Heartbreakers, not to mention the Traveling Wilburys with George Harrison and Roy Orbison. Definite high points. Then there was the fantastic Never Ending Tour bands that he initially started up with G. E. Smith and continues to this day with a rotating group of fine musicians while still staying true to the core of the Never Ending Tour sound and approach. All during this time he participated in various charity events and tributes to people and things of great importance. We saw him rise and fall and rise again.

At the end of 1996, it appeared to most Bob Dylan fans that the great years were behind him. To the general public at large, if they were even aware of who he was, he had become the punch line to a joke or a sad reminder of what the sixties used to be. Indeed, it seemed that he would be relegated to the nostalgia bin along with many other sixties heroes. But he was about to confound everyone, even his staunchest fans, when he would mount a massive comeback, both critically and commercially, in 1997. But that will have to be the subject for another book.

Acknowledgments

The following resources were invaluable to the making of this book:

Tangled Up In Tapes: A Recording History of Bob Dylan by Glen Dundas.

I Happen To Be a Swede Myself!! - Olof Bjorner's website http://www.bjorner.com

Michael Krogsgaard's *Bob Dylan: The Recording Sessions*, as serialized in *The Telegraph* and *The Bridge*. Available online at http://dobbylan.com/sessions.html

Also many thanks to all the collectors throughout the years who have kindly furnished me with tapes, because deep inside my heart, I know I can't escape.

About the Author

John Howells has been a Bob Dylan fan since at least 1970 when he first listened really hard, for the first time, to *Highway 61 Revisited* and suddenly GOT IT. His years of collecting and listening to Dylan tapes began and really got off to a start when he connected with other Dylan collectors on the nascent Internet back in the mid 1980s. Prior to that, he had to be content with buying all the vinyl bootlegs he could find at the local head shops in the town he grew up in: San Jose, California.

In 1994, he noticed that although there was a lot of information about Bob Dylan scattered throughout the Internet, there was no official Bob Dylan page or a truly comprehensive fan website, so he set out to create one that would pull together all the disparate sites into one massive resource. That website was called *Bringing It All Back Homepage*. It still exists as of this writing, but who knows for how much longer?

John is still a huge Dylan fan, but he spends most of his time these days tending to the official Graham Parker website, which can be found at http://www.grahamparker.net.

His previous book, *Skipping Reels of Rhyme: A Guide to Rare and Unreleased Bob Dylan Recordings*, was nominated for the 2019 ARSC (Association for Recorded Sound Collections) award for Excellence in Historical Recorded Sound Research.